Mytholo

A Fascinating ~~Guide to~~

Understanding Greek

Mythology, Norse Mythology,

and Egyptian Mythology

Written by the Creator of the Captivating History Series:

Matt Clayton

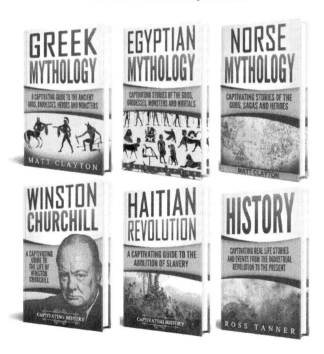

Contents

Free Bonus from Captivating History (Available for a Limited time)

Hi History Lovers!

Now you have a chance to join our exclusive history list so you can get your first history ebook for free as well as discounts and a potential to get more history books for free! Simply visit the link below to join.

Captivatinghistory.com/ebook

Also, make sure to follow us on:
Twitter: @Captivhistory
Facebook: Captivating History: @captivatinghistory

Manuscript 1:

Greek Mythology

A Fascinating Guide to Understanding the Ancient Greek Religion with Its Gods, Goddesses, Monsters and Mortals

Introduction — At the Edge of History

The ancient Greeks were explorers in many ways. They traveled to new places, creating colonies in strange lands far from their original homes. They were survivors. They were honorable thieves. They used their cunning to explore the frontiers of philosophy and they wrested from the chaos of the surrounding wilderness the building blocks of civilization.

Though the Greeks were late to the game of writing, what they wrote became an important part of our world's heritage.

Greek heroes taught us many lessons, from Homer's poetry about war and a warrior's return home, to the tales of Cadmus, Jason, Herakles and even Oedipus.

The myths of Greek heroes give us a glimpse beyond the edge of history, into the lives of very real people. How much of their tales are true, we may never know. But this book will present their tales in a new light, hopefully making their experiences a bit more real and perhaps shining a light on what may have really happened behind the distortions of time and generations of misunderstanding.

This manuscript is broken into three parts. The first will explore Greek heroes, what they were like and what they accomplished.

The second part of the book will tackle Greek religion—the gods and goddesses which establish the backdrop against which Greek legends were formed.

In the third part of the book, we take a close look at the myths of Greek monsters.

Part 1 — Greek Heroes

Chapter 1 — Honorable Thieves

There was no nation called Greece in ancient times. The Greek people possessed a common heritage and language, but they lived in separate city states that were as different as night and day. Athens, for instance, valued philosophy, wisdom and individual liberty. Sparta, on the other hand, valued strength and austerity. To the Spartans, if a child looked weak or deformed, it was left in the wilderness to die. The Spartans built a fierce, land-based military force. The Athenians built a strong naval force. When they worked together, the Greeks were a powerful enemy to whomever might threaten them. During other times, they fought amongst themselves, vying for power over their fellows.

When Greece gained a written language, its culture had already lived through a thousand years of heroism and exploits. The details of that past came down to us as myth and legend.

Those stories tell us a lot about the Greeks of prehistory. They cared about honor. They wanted to do something important with their lives. But they weren't above outright theft to achieve their otherwise honorable goals.

Jason of Iolcos was one such hero. His father, Aeson, was the rightful king of that city state, but before Jason was born, Aeson's half-brother, Pelias, seized the throne, killing everyone who could challenge him as king.

Pelias had grown up arrogant and power hungry. The knowledge that he was the son of their common mother, Tyro, and the god of the sea, Poseidon, must have made him feel he deserved to be king more than his older, half-brother. Pelias wanted to conquer the entire region surrounding Iolcos—all of Thessaly. But his selfish ambitions led to his undoing.

Ironically, Pelias spared his half-brother—the deposed king, locking him away in the dungeon. He also spared Aeson's wife, Alcimede. When she bore her husband a son, named Jason, she had her handmaidens gather around the baby and weep as if the child had been stillborn. This was sufficient to fool Pelias and to save young Jason's life.

Fearing that Pelias would one day discover and kill her son, Alcimede sent one of her handmaidens to take the infant to the centaur, Chiron. There, on Mount Pelion, nearby in southeast Thessaly, Jason was to be raised and educated by the same wise centaur who had trained Perseus, Theseus, Achilles, Herakles, Ajax and many other heroes of Greece.

Over the years, Pelias grew increasingly concerned that he would be overthrown. Perhaps his own guilt for his crimes were catching up with him. He sought the advice of an oracle who told him to beware of a man wearing only one sandal.

When Jason had become a man, he left Chiron and Mount Pelion and made his way home. On the way, he encountered an old woman standing in the shallow water of a river.

"Madam, do you need to cross?" he asked.

"Oh, bless you. Yes, but I'm afraid I might drown in the fast moving water."

"Here," replied Jason. "If you don't mind, I'll carry you across."

"You are so kind."

Halfway across the river, one of Jason's sandals became trapped in the mud. He yanked his foot loose, but the sandal stayed. Jason had been trained not to concern himself with such things. Right now, his mission was assisting the old woman. The sandal was a minor casualty of that mission.

After he finished crossing the river, the old woman thanked him and she went on her way. Jason continued on the road toward Iolcos, on the coast of the Pagasetic Gulf.

Little did Jason know, but the old woman was a disguise. She was none other than the beautiful queen of the gods, Hera—wife of Zeus, king of the gods. She'd had a longstanding grudge against Pelias. When Jason's uncle had taken the throne, he had killed his mother's stepmother, Sidero, because the old woman had abused his own mother. The old woman had sought refuge in Hera's temple, but Pelias killed her anyway, soiling the most holy place of the queen goddess. Hera made certain that Pelias would discover the prophecy of the man with one sandal. Then, she went about ensuring that Jason would lose one of his sandals during his return to Iolcos.

When Jason arrived in Iolcos, Pelias was throwing a festival in honor of his father, Poseidon, god of the seas. Everyone from throughout the region had been summoned to participate in the sacrifice to Poseidon and to indulge in the festivities which were a tribute to the sea god. When Jason entered the town, one of the guards announced his arrival as a man wearing one sandal.

Pelias was petrified with fear. This day was to be the confrontation he had long dreaded. Uncertain how to proceed and paranoid about what the young man might do, the king called the young man before him. He wanted to make a show out of this meeting, with the security of all of his own guards looking on.

"What is your name?" asked Pelias.

"My name is Jason, your highness."

"Welcome, Jason." Pelias thought for a moment and decided to be bold. "I have a riddle for you. If you were confronted by someone who would lead to your own downfall, what would you do to the man?"

Jason was surprised that the king would ask such a question without knowing who he was. His mind raced to think of an answer. He thought of all the lessons Chiron had taught him, but nothing had prepared him for such an odd query. Hera turned herself invisible and whispered in the young man's ear, telling him the answer he should give.

"Sire, I would send him in search of the Golden Fleece—the magical, healing blanket that Phrixus took to the ends of the Earth, beyond the Euxine Sea."

Pelias was stunned that this young man—this threat to his crown—would name a quest as impossible as this.

"So, your highness, did you think that I would lead to your downfall? Did you recognize your own nephew?"

This revelation stunned Pelias even further, but he had already steeled himself to this challenge. He nodded slowly and replied, "Nephew, I hereby give you this challenge by your own suggestion. You are to return with the Golden Fleece, and then I will happily turn over the throne to you."

Jason accepted the challenge. He knew not how he would accomplish such a quest, because he had never before traveled.

First, the young man looked for a ship that could carry him to the mythical land of Colchis. At the docks, he found a shipbuilder named Argo who was adding the finishing touches to a fine ship under construction. By this time, everyone had heard of Jason's confrontation with the king. They all knew of his quest.

"Sire," said Argo, "it would give me great honor to bestow on you this humble ship to help you on your quest. I have only one request—that I be allowed to be a part of your crew."

"The honor is mine, Argo," replied Jason. "This is indeed a beautiful ship. Your skills will be a welcome addition to the crew. I shall name this wonderful creation, the Argo, after its creator."

Over the next several days, Jason sent word out that he was looking for a crew to man his ship. From far and wide, many Greek heroes who lived at that time found their way to Iolcos to offer their services. Among them were Herakles, Peleus, Orpheus, the twins Castor and Pollux, Atalanta and several others. The ones selected included the Boreads—sons of the North Wind, Boreas. Jason called this elite crew, the Argonauts.

After they set sail, the Argo landed on the Isle of Lemnos, on the other side of the Aegean Sea, nestled against the coast of Asia Minor (modern Turkey), and standing in front of the Hellespont.

Lemnos was populated by a cursed group of women. They had earned the hatred of Aphrodite, goddess of love, because the women had failed in their duties of worship. In retribution, Aphrodite had made the women reek of a stench so foul that their husbands had not been able to stand being near them. Their husbands, had grown rowdy and had taken for themselves concubines from Thrace on the mainland of Greece. Because of the men's betrayal, the women had killed them in their sleep.

When the Argo arrived, the women were anxious for companionship. They seduced the Argonauts and gave birth to a new race of men—the Minyae. Even Jason participated in the frolicking, and had twins with the queen of Lemnos.

Herakles, the demigod, and strongest man alive, was able to resist the temptations of the Lemnosian women. The Argo's voyage had barely begun, and the men had become distracted by these lonely women. Finally, he was able to convince his fellow Argonauts to return to their ship.

Next, the Argo landed in the realm of the Doliones. King Cyzicus celebrated their arrival by throwing a feast in their honor. During their dinner, the king told them that they could get plenty of supplies beyond Bear Mountain. The king forgot to mention, though, that the Gegeines inhabited that land. They were a group of giants, each with six arms. While many of the

Argonauts sought their supplies, the Gegeines attacked the ship, but were fought back by Herakles. The demigod killed most of them, before Jason and the others returned.

To keep from being attacked again, Jason had the Argo shove off, despite the fact that it was mid-evening. Ironically, they ended up unwittingly landing where they had started earlier that day, near the palace of King Cyzicus. In the darkness of night, the Doliones thought they were being assaulted and attacked the Argonauts. By dawn, many Doliones lay dead, including the king. The queen, in her grief, killed herself. When the Argonauts realized that they had killed their former host, they were deeply saddened. To make up for their horrible mistake, they took the time to hold a proper funeral for the king and for those Doliones they had slaughtered.

Later that day, Jason and the Argonauts found their way across the Aegean, again, to Thrace and the kingdom of Salmydessus. When they reached the palace of King Phineas, they learned that the monarch had fallen out of favor with Zeus, king of the gods. Each day, Zeus sent harpies to snatch the food from the king's table so that he grew more and more emaciated from starvation. Jason and his crew took pity on the king and helped him destroy the giant birds with women's faces. For the first time in months, King Phineas was able to finish a meal in peace.

Phineas was so grateful, he told Jason how to find his way to Colchis, and how to pass safely through the Symplegades, or "clashing rocks."

In the narrow strait which led from the Aegean to the Euxine (Black) Sea, the Symplegades were two cliffs which came together whenever a ship passed by, crushing it between them. Phineas had suggested that Jason let loose a dove just before entering between the clashing rocks. If the dove was able to make it through, the Argonauts should row with all their might. But if the dove was crushed between the cliffs, then the Argo would not have any chance of survival between them. When Jason released the dove, he saw that it survived.

"Row, men! Row as if your lives depend on it."

The Argo barely made it past the Symplegades and with only minor damage to the stern. As they looked back at the dangerous gauntlet, they saw that the cliffs had become fused in place so that ships would now be forever capable of making it through safely.

From the Bosporus, across the northern edge of Asia Minor and to the farthest shores of the East, the Argo finally came to rest in Colchis, land of the Golden Fleece.

King Aeëtes and his people greeted Jason and his men. The travelers were treated as honored guests. The people of Colchis had so rarely received visitors from Greece or other parts of the Mediterranean, because of the dangers of the Symplegades.

At the meal in their honor, the king asked, "Why have you traveled all this way. Why do you honor us with your presence?"

"We are on a quest," replied Jason. "We seek the Golden Fleece. I am the rightful heir to the throne of Iolcos, but King Pelias requires that I return with this prize before he will relinquish the throne to me."

King Aeëtes tried not to look concerned. He swallowed with difficulty and attempted to think of a way to handle this sudden problem. These warriors were here to steal the national treasure and open conflict might result in too much bloodshed. He knew that he needed to appear accommodating to these guests, while at the same time protecting his own country from these thieves.

"I would be happy to give you the Golden Fleece, if you would first perform three tasks. This is for you, and you alone."

"What are they?" asked Jason.

"First, you must yoke our two fire-breathing bulls and plow a four-acre field with them."

Already, Jason felt overwhelmed by this impossible task. But he knew he could not leave Colchis without the Golden Fleece.

"Next, you must sow the same field with dragon's teeth. From the ground will spring an army of soldiers. You must kill them all."

"Last of all, you must kill the dragon which guards the Golden Fleece."

"Thank you, King Aeëtes. I accept your challenge. Today, I will pray to the gods and prepare myself. Tomorrow, I will perform your tasks."

In private, Jason talked to his men about the three tasks and how he might survive each of them. They heard a knock at the door and Euphemus went to answer it. Jason recognized the princess Medea, and he bade her to enter.

"Prince Jason, may I talk with you alone?"

Jason looked to his men, but did not receive any help from them. He nodded. "Okay. Men, please give us a few minutes alone."

Again, Hera had stepped in to help her hero. She had asked Aphrodite to have her son Eros aim one of his arrows at Medea and to get her to fall in love with Jason. The smitten princess was now here to betray her own people.

When the Argonauts had left, Medea turned to Jason and said, "My dearest prince, I can help you with the tasks my father gave you."

The young prince shook his head in disbelief. "Why would you betray your own people?"

"I have never met anyone like you. The men of my country are all soft and weak. They don't have the courage you exhibit. I—I think you should have the Golden Fleece."

"I still don't understand. Why are you helping me?"

"Do you believe in love?" Medea stepped closer to Jason and looked up into his eyes.

Jason could feel his heart pounding. Her perfume filled his nostrils. The beauty of her face filled his eyes with feeling. "Love? But we've barely met."

"Are you ready when opportunity presents itself? Are you brave enough to act when everything that gives your life meaning suddenly becomes possible? I've been waiting all my life for you to arrive."

Suddenly, Jason took her in his arms and kissed her passionately. She returned the kiss with an equal amount of feeling. After several minutes of passion, Jason stepped back from her and held her at arm's length. "One moment."

The young prince went to the door, opened it and looked over his men waiting there. "Back to your own rooms. We have a solution for tomorrow. I will see you all in the morning."

Again, he closed the door and turned back to Medea. "So, tell me. How can you help with my tasks?"

The following morning, the Argonauts returned to Jason's room, waiting just outside his door. A few minutes after their arrival, both Jason and Medea emerged.

They all had their breakfast, and then the royal courtiers, king, Medea and dozens of citizens went to the field that was to be plowed. Jason lathered his hands and forearms with a lotion Medea had supplied him. These protected him from being burned as he yoked the two fire-breathing bulls. Then, he easily plowed the four acres. Next, he sowed the dragon's teeth across a large part of the field. Minutes later, warriors sprang up from the earth. But before they could turn on Jason, he threw a magic stone into the midst of them and they suddenly turned on one another until only one was left. But he was exhausted and Jason easily defeated him.

Next, Jason and his men made their way to the glade where the great oak tree stood, decorated with the Golden Fleece and protected by a golden dragon. When they arrived, Medea was standing nearby. She nodded to Jason and he walked right past the dragon and took the Golden Fleece without being molested by the dragon. Medea had used her magic to put the great creature to sleep.

Quickly, Jason took the Golden Fleece and ran with the Argonauts down to the Argo and prepared to set sail. Not far behind them, the king and his soldiers chased after them.

Prince Apsyrtus, Medea's brother, was the first to arrive at the docks after the Argo had pushed off. He and his men were right behind the Argo and were quickly catching up.

Suddenly, Medea, riding the dragon, swooped down and thrashed Apsyrtus's ship, cutting it into pieces.

King Aeëtes and the rest of the men, in the other ships, had to stop to rescue the prince and his men.

Even after returning with the Golden Fleece, Pelias resisted living up to his end of the bargain. In the meantime, Medea used her magic to make Jason's father younger and stronger, despite his years wasting away in the dungeon.

When Pelias's daughters saw this, they asked Medea to do the same for their father. Medea suggested, instead, that their father could go even further and become a young man, again. She took an old goat, cut it into pieces and tossed the pieces into a cauldron. Out jumped a young lamb.

So, the daughters cut up their father, tossed the pieces into the same cauldron, and waited for Medea to do her magic. But she refused. Pelias's son, Acastus, used his soldiers to drive Jason and Medea from Iolcos for his father's murder.

Understanding Jason's Story

Ironically, Jason and Medea did not murder Pelias. His own daughters had killed him. And Acastus's father had betrayed his oath to Jason by not turning over the kingdom to him promptly upon Jason's return. Pelias had lied. But the kingdom was lawfully Jason's anyway, with his father's forced retirement. Pelias had stolen the kingdom from Aeson, Jason's father. Pelias had been a thief and Jason had become a thief in order to resolve that earlier theft.

Jason had added to the crimes of the story by his intention of stealing the Golden Fleece from the people of Colchis. And the Greeks thought this was perfectly okay to do. Ultimately, Jason did not have to steal it, because Medea had betrayed her own people to help Jason. But what if King Aeëtes had refused to give the Golden Fleece to Jason? Would Jason have murdered the king and his soldiers to force his will in the matter?

If Jason had merely demanded that the throne be returned to his father or to himself, Pelias likely would have had Jason killed. For what is one more murder by Pelias after so many others? In the end, Pelias lost all honor by his selfishness and lying.

Jason started out as a righteous hero, headed toward reclaiming his lost heritage. But he ended up betraying all that. For all he had promised to Medea for helping him, and for bearing him two beautiful sons, he asked the princess of Corinth for her hand in marriage. The young prince had been blinded by political greed—a hunger for power. By marrying the princess, he figured he'd have an extra advantage that he could not have enjoyed by being weighted down by Medea, his foreign princess. Jason had stolen the Golden Fleece in an honorable fashion, passing the tasks given to him by King Aeëtes. But in the end, Jason died poor and alone because of his betrayal of Medea.

To the Greeks, some actions are dishonorable. Stealing for a righteous cause seems to have been one act they held as honorable. But lying and betraying promises went too far for both Pelias and Jason.

Chapter 2 — Legends of Pride

The Greeks had a unique advantage over most other nations. Though their land was relatively poor compared to the Nile Valley or Mesopotamia, the fact that so many of their cities were close to the sea gave them a psychological advantage over the people of other nations.

Robert C. Lamm and Neil M. Cross, in their book, *The Humanities in Western Culture, Ed. IX,* comment on the Aegean heritage given to the world by the Greeks. "There appear to be several constants that run through all cultures: seaports are, by their nature, urban centers, cities that are more receptive to change than are rural areas; those who travel are generally more open to innovative ideas and foreign customs than those who habitually stay home, especially farmers. In many cases there seems to be a consistent equation: the farther a person is from the seacoast, the more resistant that person will be to change and new ideas.

"Throughout history, civilizations have evolved to levels that were largely determined by their developments in urban living, commerce, trade, and travel. Considering all these factors, it is hardly surprising—much less miraculous—that civilizations in the Aegean reached such high levels."

First the Mycenaean Greeks and then the Dorians (like Sparta) and Ionians (like Athens) took advantage of the high mix of land and sea throughout the region. A large part of Ancient Greece consisted of islands, peninsulas and coastlines.

With an abundance of port cities and relatively poor farmland, the Greeks became traders, travelers and colonists. At the height of Ancient Greek civilization, before Alexander the Great conquered a large part of the known world, the Greek world included coastal settlements from Eastern Spain to the Eastern Black Sea. The cities of Odessa, Ukraine and Marseilles,

France were both originally Greek colonies. So was Byzantium (modern Instanbul).

With so much travel going on through the Greek realm, it's no wonder that they had many legends of heroes and great accomplishments.

Legend of Cadmus, Founder of Thebes, Greece

Cadmus was not a Greek, originally. He was a Phoenician—a prince of Tyre, in the Levant.

His story starts with the abduction of his sister, Europa. She was quite lovely, and Zeus, king of the gods, took a liking to her. Zeus transformed himself into a white bull and walked amongst the herds of Tyre's King Agenor. It just so happened that Europa had been picking flowers nearby. She saw the pure white bull and became enamored with its beauty. She caressed the side of it and then climbed on top of it, all to the dismay of her handmaidens. At that moment, Zeus, in possession of the damsel he most desired, ran down to the sea so quickly that Europa dared not dismount. Then Zeus swam to Crete and transformed back into a human-like form, telling the princess of his true identity. She ended up bearing

Zeus many children, because he came back to Crete many times to visit her. The king of gods gave her many gifts, including a necklace fashioned by Hephaestus, the god of fire and metallurgy. The other gifts included, for her protection, Laelaps, a dog which never failed to find its prey, Talos, a mechanical winged man which flew around Crete three times a day to keep watch, and a magical javelin which never missed its mark.

So deeply did Zeus love Europa that he took the image of the bull with which he had first seduced the princess and turned it into the constellation of Taurus, the bull.

Back in Tyre, the king and queen sent their son, Cadmus to go find his sister and to return her safely home.

After long months of searching, Cadmus finally consulted the Oracle at Delphi. The seers told him that Europa was safe and quite happy with Zeus. So, he should give up his search. But they recommended that Cadmus take up another quest in order to fulfill his destiny as founder of Thebes.

The Oracle told him to find a black and white cow and to follow the creature until it came to rest. There, they should build their new city.

So, Cadmus left Delphi with his men and searched nearby for a black and white cow. After a couple of days, they found one, just as described by the Oracle. For two more days, they followed the bovine creature until it came to rest near a river. There, they slaughtered the cow as a sacrifice to the gods and in preparation for consecrating the ground where they would build their city.

To complete their sacrifice, Cadmus sent half of his men to get water from the river. But after nearly an hour, his men did not return. The prince then sent the other half of his men to find out what had happened. When they did not return, Cadmus went himself to investigate.

At the edge of an open field, next to the river, Cadmus spotted a golden dragon sitting on the ground. In the field before it were the dead bodies of all his men. Some had been gruesomely hacked to death.

Outraged, Cadmus attacked the dragon with his sword and knocked out some of its teeth. The dragon shuddered and smoke poured out from its snout. Suddenly, several warriors appeared and began fighting amongst themselves. They hacked at each other with their swords, and finally only a handful were left, too tired to fight any more.

Cadmus was able to communicate with them enough to convince them to join in his building of the new city. As they spoke, the dragon silently lifted into the sky and flew away.

The Illiad

Ancient Greek past is divided into several periods. The first is that of myth and legend. The second is the Archaic period from whence the first Greek writing of any note comes to us. The two most famous writings of this period have been attributed to a man named Homer. We know little about him. In fact, it's quite possible that the writing was actually done by more than one person and the works collected by others. The Iliad tells the story of the ten-year war of the Greek city states against Troy (Ilion). The Odyssey tells the story of the ten-year voyage home of King Odysseus and his men. These writings tell of two events which occurred during the period of myth and legend.

For many years, scientists felt that the story of Troy was nothing more than myth—a story made up by Homer. Ironically even today, scientists are quick to dismiss ideas that lay outside of their teachings and experience. They use logical fallacies to put such notions away, effectively refusing to investigate. So, it took amateur investigators to unravel the mystery, because the professionals "knew better" than to try.

A Scottish journalist named Charles Maclaren claimed, in 1822, to have identified the true location of Troy at a large hill named Hisarlik in western Turkey. Forty-four years later, Frank Calvert, whose family owned half of the hill, made detailed inspections of the land. Heinrich Schliemann visited Frank Calvert in 1868 and was so impressed by what Calvert had done that he financed a more extensive dig. Regrettably, Schliemann took credit for the finds. And professional archaeologists later condemned Schliemann's amateurish damage to the site.

So, it seems that the myth of the Trojan War may have been, in part, based on fact.

According to myth, the roots of the tragic war can be found in the lust of both Zeus and Poseidon for Thetis, a sea nymph and goddess of water. When Zeus learned that the son born of Thetis would be greater than his father, Zeus was concerned that his desired sexual exploits with Thetis would result in his own dethroning. The king of gods then warned his brother of the same prophecy and the two of them made a pact to avoid sex with Thetis, lest it lead to their undoing. Instead, they plotted to have Thetis marry a mortal. They chose Peleus.

But Peleus asked and Thetis refused. Proteus, one of the ancient sea gods, told Peleus that he needed to catch Thetis while she was sleeping. He should bind her so she could not change shape into a serpent, raging lioness, water or flame. Thus, Thetis was forced to agree to their marriage. It's interesting to note that kidnapping was considered okay to the Greeks, but breaking a promise was considered dishonorable.

Zeus wanted their marriage to be an event no one would soon forget. He picked a garden near Chiron's cave on Mount Pelion. All of the gods, goddesses and demigods were invited, yet one goddess was expressly forbidden to attend. That was Eris, goddess of discord. And no one would ever want a troublemaker at a party, especially a wedding party.

Eris was not pleased at being left out. She took one of the golden apples of Hesperides, inscribed on it, "To the most beautiful," and tossed it over the garden wall.

But who would claim to be the recipient of the Golden Apple? Who would be vain enough to think that she was the most beautiful female mentioned in the inscription. Eris had lived up to her name, creating discord despite having not been invited.

Hera, Aphrodite and Athena each claimed the Golden Apple. To settle this dispute, they called upon Zeus to judge who among them was the most fair. But the king of gods was too wise to get involved in this no-win scenario. He knew that the two losers would end up hating him for a very long time. So, Zeus chose the wise and fair judge, Prince Paris of Troy.

After the wedding party, the three goddesses bathed in a spring near Mount Ida, not far from Troy, and then presented themselves to the prince while he tended to his flock of sheep.

Paris found it impossible to choose and begged their forgiveness.

Desperate to win, each goddess in turn, stripped off her clothes, stood naked before the young prince, and attempted to bribe him. Hera told Paris that she would make him king of all Europe and Asia. Athena offered to give him superior skill and wisdom in war. And

Aphrodite offered to Paris the love of the most beautiful woman in the world.

"But how?" asked Paris. "The most beautiful woman is Helen, wife of Menelaus."

"Am I not the goddess of love?"

Paris gave the Golden Apple to Aphrodite and thus set upon the path to war and to his own city's destruction.

Helen's father had been so worried that his daughter's great beauty would cause war to break out amongst the Greek city states and amongst the dozens of suitors from those royal houses. He obtained an oath from each of the suitors that they would defend the honor of Helen's marriage after her father had made his choice.

When Paris later visited Sparta, Helen immediately fell in love with him and left her husband willingly. Menelaus was outraged that the Trojan prince would insult Sparta by stealing its queen. King Menelaus contacted his brother, King Agamemnon and then the others who had sworn to protect Helen's marriage to Menelaus. He encouraged them to honor their oaths. And thus began the Greek war against Troy.

Homer's Iliad covers only a few weeks of the ten-year conflict, but it mentions in passing many of the back story elements.

After many deaths on both sides, the Greeks suddenly disappeared from the battlefield. In their place, before the great gates of Troy, a giant, wooden horse stood.

The Trojan people were overjoyed that they had defeated the Greeks and then they wheeled into their city the tribute left behind.

After their celebration had wound down and the people had gone to bed, tired and happy, Greek soldiers opened a secret hatch on the bottom of the wooden horse. They crept to the city gates and flung them open to the waiting Greek army.

In one night of Greek cleverness, Troy had lost the war. Today, the term "Trojan horse" refers to a sneak attack hidden inside something more pleasant.

The Odyssey

The thousands of Greeks warriors who remained after the fall of Troy, each took their own ships and returned home. But during their voyage home, King Odysseus and his men were blown off course by a storm.

Homer's Odyssey tells of the ten-year struggle of Odysseus and his men to return home to Ithaca—an island at what was then the far western edge of Greek territory.

When Menelaus sent word to all the former suitors of Helen, Odysseus pretended to be crazy. He attempted to plow his own field using both a donkey and an ox yoked together. This proved to be highly inefficient, because the two animals have entirely different strides. And Odysseus threw salt into the furrows instead of seed. He had received a prediction that, if he went, he would be delayed for many years in his return home. Naturally, Odysseus did not want to leave his wife, Penelope and their newborn son, Telemachus.

Agamemnon, brother to Menelaus, sent Palamedes to verify or disprove the king's madness. Agamemnon's envoy borrowed Penelope's child and placed it before the plow and that stopped Odysseus, showing that he was indeed, quite sane.

The war lasted ten years. And, as Odysseus had feared, the journey home lasted another ten. When he finally returned to his family, Telemachus was a young man of twenty.

But many of the other Greek kings were thankful that Odysseus was with them, because of his wise counsel and his brilliant idea for the great wooden horse.

On his journey home, all twelve of his ships find their way out of a storm and into the land of the lotus eaters—drug addicts who enticed the king and his men to eat their delicious lotus plant. The narcotic effect made them lose any interest in returning home. Through sheer strength of will, Odysseus was able to force his men back to their ships and they manned the oars to put some distance between them and the seductive lotus plants. Scholars place this land just off the coast of Tunisia, on Djerba Island, or in coastal Libya.

From there, Odysseus and his twelve ships sailed north, past Sicily and into the Tyrrhenian Sea. In dire need of provisions, they pulled up to a small island and went ashore. In a nearby cave, they found a large supply of provisions and thought themselves to be lucky. Moments later, a giant Cyclops came into the cave, herding a flock of sheep, and rolled a large stone into place, blocking the exit.

"Hello," said Odysseus. "Please forgive our intrusion, but we are your guests—weary travelers from afar. As is the custom, we ask that you share your food with us."

"I, Polyphemus, do not believe in such customs." The Cyclops promptly picked up one of the Greek warriors and took a bite out of him. In two more bites, the man was gone. Then, the giant ate one more. In the dim light of the cave's one fire, the giant could see the remainder of the warriors cowering against the wall.

"I will save all of you for later," said the Cyclops.

The following morning, the Cyclops ate two more warriors. Before Polyphemus could take his sheep out to pasture, Odysseus struck up a conversation with the one-eyed giant.

After they had talked for a few minutes, the giant asked, "What is your name? Please tell me. If you do, I'll give you a guest prize to make it worth your while."

Odysseus thought carefully for a moment, guided by the quiet whispers of Athena, goddess of wisdom. "My name is Nobody. And what is this prize of which you spoke?"

"Well, Nobody, I will save you for last. You will have a few more days of life than your comrades."

"Thank you, Polyphemus. I noticed that you have some wine. Perhaps that would help stave off the heartburn. We Greeks can be hard to digest."

"Hmm-mm. Good idea, Nobody. A little wine would be delightful about now."

Polyphemus picked up the barrel, removed the stopper and drank deeply, gulping down the intoxicating liquor.

Odysseus continued his conversation, encouraging the Cyclops to drink more so as to enjoy his lunch that much more. Before long, Polyphemus was so drunk, he fell asleep.

"Quickly," said Odysseus. "Help me sharpen this pole." The Greeks whittled the end of a long, wooden pole so that it now had a strong, sharp point. They hardened it in the fire and then thrust the point into the giant's sleeping eye.

Polyphemus shrieked in pain and scrambled around the cave, attempting to find any of the Greeks, but they were able to stay just out of reach. The giant bellowed and shouted, then picked up things at random and threw them, hoping to hit one or more of the men. But nothing he did gave him satisfaction.

Odysseus taunted him that his sheep would now go hungry, because Polyphemus could not see to take his flock out to pasture.

Taking this as a dare, Polyphemus carefully opened the cave entrance, and called to his sheep, feeling of their coats to make certain that none of the Greeks were trying to escape. Then he rolled the great stone back into place to keep the Greeks inside.

Because the Cyclops could not see, he did not notice that each man had hidden underneath a sheep, clutching to its fleece to make their escape. Outside, they simply rolled away from the sheep and quietly made their way back toward their ships.

Outside, Polyphemus encountered one of his fellow Cyclops.

"Polyphemus, what happened to your eye?"

"Nobody did this to me."

"But how did it happen?"

"Are you deaf? I told you that Nobody did this to me."

"Yes, I heard you. It's okay if you don't want to talk about it." In the distance, the Greek warriors were boarding their ships. "Oh, my! So many men! If only we were closer, we could feast on human flesh. But they're getting away."

"What? More men? I have some in my cave. Unless—" Polyphemus stumbled toward his friend's voice. "Please, point to them for me."

Immediately, the Cyclops ran in the direction of the Greek ships which were now pulling up anchor.

"Nobody!" Polyphemus called out. "Is that you? How did you escape?"

Odysseus felt suddenly impulsive. Athena had been helping the king most of his life, but now she felt a pang of disappointment that she could not prevent the king's next action. Because of his rage over the loss of his men, and because of his own ego, the king of Ithaca yelled back to the wounded Cyclops, "I fooled you, you arrogant, foul creature. Know this: that I, Odysseus of Ithaca did spoil your eye for the murder of my men. May you spend the remainder of your days in despair."

At the sound of the king's voice, Polyphemus could tell the direction and distance. He fell to his knees, scrambling around the ground until he found a boulder. With fierce strength, he plucked it from the ground and threw it in the direction of the king's ship, but his blind aim missed the ship altogether.

As the ships made their way from the island, Polyphemus cried out to his father, Poseidon. "Father,

I have been wounded by Odysseus, king of Ithaca. Avenge me for I have been blinded."

If only Odysseus had remained "Nobody" in the mind of Polyphemus, Poseidon may never have known who had injured his son. Poseidon made certain that the king would be delayed in his return home and that he would lose all his men.

The lost Greeks found their way to the island of Aeolus, god of the winds. There, the king's ship was outfitted with a bag of winds which would blow their ships back to Ithaca. But Poseidon whispered into the ear of one of the king's men that the bag contained gold. In a fit of momentary greed, the man opened the bag just as they came within sight of home. The resulting storm blew them all the way back to the home of Aeolus. Outraged at their return, Aeolus refused to help them any more.

From there, the Greek ships make landfall on southern Corsica, in the realm of the Laestrygonians who also like eating men. After their escape, they encounter Circe, the witch, on the western coast of the Italian peninsula. She was the perfect hostess until her spell turned half of his men into pigs. Hermes, the messenger god intervened and gave Odysseus a potion which made him temporarily immune to Circe's magic. Thus, the Ithacan king was able to force Circe to restore his men. She did so, but Circe admitted that she loved Odysseus and wanted very much for him to stay with her. His men stay with Circe for a year, with Odysseus taking part of that time to visit the underworld, whereupon he learns of many events, including the murder of his friend, King Agamemnon, and his wife's troubles with suitors.

Finally, the king of Ithaca is convinced by his men to return home. Circe tells Odysseus about some of the dangers which remain on his voyage and how to survive them.

While passing the land of the Sirens, Odysseus has his men plug their ears with bees wax so they will not steer their ships toward the rocks. But Odysseus has his men tie him to the mast of his own ship so he can witness the magical song of the Sirens and live to tell about it.

Then, the Greek ships navigate the narrow strait between Sicily and Italy—between the six-headed monster, Scylla, and the deadly whirlpool, Charybdis. Despite their care, the Scylla is able to grab one of their oars and pulls the ship close enough to snatch up six men.

Next, Odysseus and his remaining ships land on the island of Thrinacia to replenish their depleted provisions. Some of his men ignored the warnings of Circe and took some of the cattle there belonging to the sun god, Helios.

Outraged, Helios demanded that Zeus punish the Greek warriors for their theft. "If you don't," said Helios, "I'll make the sun shine in the underworld, instead of the land of the living."

Zeus didn't like the idea of living in darkness, or moving to the underworld, so he used his lightning to stir up a storm, crashing all of the Greek ships, killing all but Odysseus.

Weak, battered and hungry, Odysseus washed up on the shore of Ogygia Island, where he remained a prisoner and lover of Calypso for seven years. He might well have stayed there for the rest of his life had it not been for the help of Hermes, demanding that she release Odysseus from her spell.

Odysseus took a small boat and again became shipwrecked on the island of the Phaeacians (modern Corfu). There, he tells his story and they agree to help him get home secretly so as not to alert the suitors threatening his wife.

On his way home, he encounters his son Telemachus and has him promise to keep his identity a secret until they have killed all the suitors who have abused his wife and son.

Disguised as a wandering beggar, the king wandered into his own palace and was quickly abused by the suitors. Penelope did not recognize her husband in his clever disguise—a camouflage devised by Athena. She told all who were nearby that she will marry the one who can string her husband's bow and shoot an arrow through the shafts of twelve axes.

One by one, each suitor took up the bow—a gift to Odysseus from the god, Apollo—but each failed to string the bow. Finally, Odysseus, still disguised as a beggar, strung the bow and let loose an arrow with such force that it easily sliced through all twelve axe shafts. Then, before the surprise could clear from the suitors' minds, the king let loose the rest of his arrows, killing many of the suitors where they sat, while his son and servant bolted the doors. When the slaughter was complete, Odysseus and his son returned to Penelope.

"How do I know you're not some apparition from the gods?" she asked.

"Test me, my love."

"All right, then. Move our bed to the other side of our bedroom."

Odysseus let out a tired laugh and then reminded his wife, "But my darling, one of the bedposts is a tree rooted to the ground itself, just as I had built it so many years ago."

Deeper Meaning?

Homer's Iliad tells of a war over a queen's infidelity. But the Greeks were always concerned about honor and how their actions would appear, not only to their fellow Greeks, but to posterity. Could the Trojan War have been more about their own selfishness? Troy stood at the entrance to the Black Sea. It controlled that traffic. What if the Greeks were jealous of that control? What if they wanted to eliminate Troy in order to conquer the Black Sea for themselves?

The story of Helen's escape to Troy may or may not have been true. But even if it were true, it could have been orchestrated by Menelaus and the other Greeks in order to eliminate their competition in Troy. Such is the hypothesis of Rod Martin, Jr. concerning this ancient Greek tale. Lying to achieve an honorable goal was considered also honorable. So, the Greeks could have lied about their reason for going to war against Troy. They deeply respected cleverness and cunning.

Part 2 — Greek Religion

Chapter 3 — The Burdens of Selfishness and Hubris

In the Ancient Greek religion, the universe was originally ruled by Chaos (emptiness). Like so many other primitive religions, Chaos needed to be tamed and the early gods established a foundation from which all of creation could persist.

Gaia (mother Earth) sprang into existence from Chaos. She gave birth to Uranus (heaven) and Pontus (ocean).

In the Greek religion, even the gods felt vulnerable. They were constantly battling against various kinds of chaos or turmoil. One of the recurring themes involved fathers who feared or loathed their children.

Gaia took her son, Uranus, as her lover and gave birth to a host of additional gods, who later became known as the Titans. After the Titans, Gaia gave birth to the Cyclopes (3 one-eyed giants) and Hecatonchires (3 hundred-handed giants). Uranus despised these six youngest children and locked them up in Tartarus (underworld), much to Gaia's dismay.

Cronus volunteered to help his mother get her youngest children out of prison. She gave him a massive sickle with which to castrate his father. Cronus ambushed his father and crippled him. But Cronus also despised his younger brothers and ran them back into Tartarus at his first opportunity. Gaia felt betrayed.

Cronus took his sister, Rhea, as his wife and she gave him many children. But Cronus, fearful that his own children would do to him what he had done to his own father, he swallowed each of them whole. When Rhea had Zeus, she put a boulder in the infant's swaddling clothes and presented this to her husband. He didn't take the time to look and merely gulped it down.

Rhea had her only remaining son raised away from court so that Cronus would not discover the trickery.

When Zeus had come of age, he wanted revenge for the deaths of his older siblings. His wife, Metis, was the wisest of the gods and she suggested that Zeus become the cupbearer to Cronus. Into his drink, Zeus should put a powerful herb which would cause Cronus to vomit up the children he had swallowed so many years before. And it worked. After getting his brothers and sisters back, Zeus set free the Cyclopes and Hecatonchires so that the younger gods would have a fighting chance against the older Titans.

The Cyclopes were so thankful at being set free, they fashioned a lightning bolt for Zeus, a helmet of invisibility for Hades, and a massive trident for Poseidon.

After ten years of fighting, the younger gods conquered Cronus and his old guard, and placed the lot of them in Tartarus—the underworld prison.

After settling into their new roles as masters of the universe, these younger gods, now ruling from Mount Olympus, divided up their areas of responsibilities. Zeus would be their king and hold dominion over the skies. Poseidon would take the seas, and Hades would rule over the underworld.

But one day, Zeus was told of a prophecy, that his children by Metis would overthrow him as king of the gods. Fearing for his own personal chaos, the new king of gods did the only selfish thing he could do. He swallowed Metis whole, despite the fact that she was already pregnant.

Zeus would have six other wives, many concubines and lovers, and dozens of children. A man's wife was supposed to do his bidding and to remain faithful, but Zeus did as he pleased.

Thus, when bad things happened to good people, the Greeks could blame their bad fortune on conflicts between the gods. An insult would not go unnoticed and the damaged pride of one god or goddess would not go unpunished. Or a mortal child fathered by Zeus, or their mother, would be tortured and hounded by Hera, Zeus's seventh and most jealous wife.

So, the Greek gods and goddesses had very human frailties and the world suffered because of them.

Chapter 4 — The Ages of Man

The earliest age of man was called the Golden Age. This was during the time of Cronus. His rule brought great prosperity to the world and the gods lived amongst the humans.

The Silver Age came during the rule of Zeus. When the humans refused to worship Zeus, he destroyed them. The few humans who were sturdy enough to survive were warriors. Because these men were destructive, Zeus decided to destroy them, as well. And thus, the Bronze Age of man came to an end, because Zeus sent a great flood to rid the world of them.

Two people survived that great flood. They were named Deucalion and Pyrrah. On the command of Zeus to repopulate the world, these two turned stones into humans. The hardness of the stones thus came to represent the hardness of their lives in the new Heroic Age. To Zeus's delight, the men of this age held great honor and humble worship of the gods.

But like all artifacts of the physical world, the Heroic Age died out and Zeus created yet another group of humans. This was the Iron Age, the most brutal age of them all.

Chapter 5 — Morals of the Gods

The Greek gods did not have the highest of morals—not by modern standards. In this, the Greek religion offered its adherents a bitter taste of reality. Being good, honorable or even clever did not guarantee a positive outcome.

Zeus had all his ladies. And in the wake of his infidelity, a great deal of suffering was born.

Zeus Giving Birth to a New Kind of Chaos

The king of gods was a vindictive jerk. If someone fell onto Zeus's bad side, the unlucky man or woman might end up being tortured forever. There was no leniency or mercy. There was no nurturing spirit to improve the attitudes of those in his charge. For the slightest infraction, Zeus wanted revenge. And when Zeus did what he felt like doing, people—and even some of the gods—got hurt because of it.

Sisyphus earned the wrath of Zeus by too much scheming to kill his own brother, Salmoneus. The wayward mortal had consulted an oracle to see how he could best be rid of his brother. The seer told him to marry his niece, Tyro, and that her children would then kill their uncle and grandfather. When Tyro found out what her husband's plans had been all along, she murdered her own son and married Cretheus, king of Iolcos. But then she fell in love with Enipeus, a river god, who spurned her advances. When Poseidon took a liking to her, he disguised himself as Enipeus and slept with her. She bore him two children—Pelias (the half brother Aeson, evil uncle of Jason), and Neleus (future king of Pylos). Sisyphus earned a place in Tantalus where he had to roll a large boulder up a hill. But every time he accomplished the deed, the boulder would roll back down. So, he was doomed for eternity to perform a task that would immediately be undone.

Tantalus had been given the rare privilege to be invited to dine at Olympus, amongst the gods. To impress the gods, Tantalus offered up his own son as a sacrifice. He cut up the young boy and made a stew out of the bits and pieces. Instead of admiration for his sacrifice, the gods were disgusted. Instead, they restored the boy to life and Zeus condemned Tantalus to Tartarus. His special place was to have his feet stuck in one place with a fruit tree above him and a pool of water below. Whenever he reached up in hunger to pluck the fruit, the branches would pull back, just out of reach. Whenever he kneeled to satisfy his thirst, the water would recede from his lips. From his name, we have the English word "tantalize"—perpetual temptation without any satisfaction.

Prometheus ran afoul of Zeus for daring to give fire to the mortals of Earth. For the kindness of Prometheus, he was rewarded by being chained to a mountain. Every day, a giant eagle would come to eat his liver. Because Prometheus was a Titan, he was immortal. At night, he would heal, and the next day, the painful process would start all over again. His fate would have been perpetual torment, had it not been for the cleverness and heroism of Herakles. With his massive strength, he killed the giant eagle and broke the chains which bound the Titan.

Part 3 — Greek Monsters

Chapter 6 — Typhon and Echidna

Gaia had taken many lovers after her son, Cronus, castrated her son and husband Uranus. When she took her brother, Tartarus, as lover, their one child was Typhon, the deadliest monster of all time.

Typhon took Echidna as his wife. She was half woman, half snake, and she bore him many monstrous children.

Despite the wrongs committed by her children, Gaia felt heartbroken that her grandchildren had locked the Titans in Tartarus. She spoke to Typhon and asked that he battle with Zeus and then to set the Titans free. And Typhon agreed.

With a form consisting of a massive trunk from which sprang a hundred snake heads, even the gods of Olympus trembled and fled. From every mouth, nostril and eye, giant flames would flash out at Typhon's enemies. And the monster's bellowing screams were akin to dozens of volcanoes erupting all at once.

Battle hardened after having spent ten years defeating the Titans, Zeus was no pushover. With his first volley of lightning, he seared off all of Typhon's ugly heads. The monster fell over in shock at the sudden loss. Zeus jumped on the beast and beat him again and again and again. When Typhon had been pummeled nearly to death, Zeus dragged the creature's hideous carcass into Tartarus (Typhon's father) and locked him away forever.

Echidna and her children quivered in fear that the same might happen to them.

Chapter 7 — Perseus and Cetus

King Acrisius of Argos wanted a son, but the Oracle at Delphi told him that he would never have one. Instead, they told him that his own grandson, by his daughter Danaë, would ultimately lead to the king's death.

Terrified, the king locked up his daughter so that no man would ever touch her. But Zeus, king of the gods, had taken a liking to her and descended into her prison as a shower of golden rain. When she gave birth to a baby boy, named Perseus, Acrisius locked them both in a box and threw the box into the sea. Days later, mother and son landed on Serifos Island

and were befriended by a fisherman named Dictys, brother to the island's king.

When Perseus came of age, the king of Serifos, Polydectes, tricked the young demigod into a deadly quest—to bring back the head of Medusa. One look at the vile creature's face would turn a man to stone.

Being a beloved son of Zeus, Perseus had help from many of the gods and goddesses—winged sandals from Hermes, a polished shield from Athena, a helmet of invisibility from Hades, and an unbreakable sword from his father, Zeus.

With these divine gifts, Perseus was able to cut off Medusa's head without himself being turned to stone. He even had a special sack in which to store the hideous head.

On his way home, Perseus encountered a major distraction. King Cepheus of Ethiopia had chained his own daughter, Andromeda, to a rock so that she could be sacrificed to Poseidon's pet monster, Cetus.

One look at Andromeda and Perseus was smitten with her beauty. In order to save the fair princess, he climbed to the top of the rock and waited. When Cetus emerged from the sea to devour the young woman, Perseus closed his eyes and withdrew Medusa's head from his bag. Immediately, Cetus turned to stone and Andromeda was saved.

Before returning to Serifos, Perseus stopped in Argos to visit his evil grandfather. When Perseus told the old man who he was and what he had done, the king called him a liar. "How dare you lie to your king. You could not have obtained Medusa's head. That's impossible."

The young hero shook his head in disgust and opened the sack one last time, fulfilling the oracle's prophecy.

Chapter 8 — Herakles and His Labors

Zeus was a serial adulterer. Not only had he had six wives before his sister, Hera, but he had dozens of other lovers—both divine and mortal. One of the mortal mistresses was Alcmene, wife of Theban General Amphitryon. Zeus presented himself to Alcmene in the form of her husband, and made her pregnant with a son. That same evening, Amphitryon returned from war and made love to his wife, making her pregnant with another son.

Zeus's wife, Hera, despised the children of her husband's infidelity. When she heard that another demigod son would be born, Hera coerced her husband to agree that a descendent of Perseus would become high king of all the land. Two ancestors of Perseus were about to be born. She knew that Eurystheus was soon to be born, and, wanting to cheat Herakles (born Alcides) of the position as high king, she went to speed up the birth of Eurystheus. She also commanded Ilithyia, goddess of childbirth, to cross her legs, thus slowing down the delivery of Alcmene's two boys—twins from two fathers.

Alcmene's servant girl lied to Ilithyia. "My lady has already delivered her two boys."

In great relief, Ilithyia relaxed and thus allowed the birth to proceed as normal.

The general's wife, however, knew what was going on. She feared that Hera would harm her family if she found out that the young demigod had been born. To save the rest of her family, she left the young demigod out in the open to die of exposure.

Goddess Athena took pity on her half-brother and took him up to Olympus. When she arrived at the home of the gods, Hera did not recognize the young infant. She took pity on him and suckled him. But the young demigod was so strong in his sucking that he tortured the queen goddess. In agony, she ripped the infant from her breast and the milk which had been gushing out sprayed across the heavens, creating the Milky Way.

Because the infant had tasted divine milk, he developed super powers of great strength.

Athena recognized that any further aid on Olympus was likely not possible, so she returned the infant to his mortal parents. There, they raised both the demigod, Alcides, and his mortal, twin brother Iphicles.

Later, in an attempt to quiet Hera's rage, the young son of Zeus was renamed Herakles in the queen goddess's honor.

Hera was so outraged by this flawed attempt to quell her anger, that she sent two vipers into the children's room. Iphicles, of course, was terrified. Herakles grabbed a snake in each hand and squeezed the life out of them. Later, a servant found the young demigod playing with the dead snakes as if they were toys.

When Herakles came of age, he married Megara of Thebes, King Creon's daughter. The young couple soon had two beautiful children.

The young man's happiness was like a thorn in Hera's eye. She put a spell on the young man so that he murdered his own children.

After Herakles had been cured of his temporary madness, he sought advice from the Oracle at Delphi, not realizing that the seer was guided by Hera—his nemesis.

The Oracle told Herakles that he could regain his honor by going to his distant cousin, High King Eurystheus and serving him for ten years. Herakles was to do anything that the king required of him. Ironically, Herakles would have been the High King, but Hera had cheated him of that.

Eurystheus gave his archenemy ten impossible tasks, but once they were done, the king found reason to dismiss two of the accomplishments on technicalities that had not been specified in advance. On a whim, he gave Herakles two more chores, making it twelve labors in all. The labors were,

1. Kill the Nemean Lion.
2. Kill the Lernaean Hydra with its 9 heads.
3. Retrieve the Golden Hind of goddess Artemis.
4. Imprison the Erymanthian Boar.

5. Cleanse the Augean stables all within one twenty-four hour period.
6. Kill the Stymphalian Birds.
7. Imprison the Cretan Bull.
8. Take the Mares of Diomedes.
9. Steal the girdle of Hippolyta, the Amazon queen.
10. Round up the cattle of Geryon the monster.
11. Take the golden apples of the Hesperides.
12. Enslave the Cerberus and return to Eurystheus with it.

After these labors, Herakles went on to have many other adventures, including joining Jason and his Argonauts in their quest to steal the Golden Fleece.

Conclusion

I hope this work on Greek mythology has helped to give you a deeper understanding of Greek myth—its heroes, monsters, gods and goddesses.

If you want to further explore our past and how the Greeks played a vital role in creating civilization, I recommend you continue to study Greek history. Find out more about the individual gods and goddesses. In all those details, you might find patterns that may reveal clues to what really happened so very long ago.

Manuscript 2:

Norse Mythology

A Fascinating Guide to Understanding the Sagas, Gods, Heroes, and Beliefs of the Vikings

Introduction

The Vikings of Norse poetry and saga were a fearless lot, and their tales were frequently tragic. Some, if not all, of the myths were based on real people and real events. These heroes accomplished many fantastic feats, some of them even documented by their enemies.

The Vikings were born out of an age of hardship. Tales of their earliest raids come to us from the 790s, during the early European Middle Ages. This was a period of dangerous iciness as the thousand-year climate cycle dipped to the coldest our world had experienced in 7,000 years. No doubt, the punishing cold for these people of Northern Europe helped to dispel any complacency they may have felt during the warmer, mid-Holocene epoch. Death was sitting on their doorstep and the weak and timid would have died from the change in climate. Only the strong and cunning would survive.

The Vikings began to raid villages farther south, conquering parts of what is modern day Netherlands, France, England and Ireland. The Vikings also became adventurers and traders, taking their wares as far as Byzantium, Baghdad and Kiev.

Generally speaking, the Norwegian clans spread throughout the western portions of Europe—Scotland, Iceland, and even into the Americas in Greenland and Canada's Newfoundland. The Danes attacked and settled in England and France's Normandy. In fact, the Normans who later conquered Anglo-Saxon England and who became the British aristocracy were originally of Viking blood. The Swedes traveled East and established the Kievan Rus' in what is today the Ukraine. And these Norsemen even ruled over the southern Mediterranean island of Sicily. But even these rules of thumb do not cover all of Norse history. Some Norwegians also traveled to the Slavic lands of East Europe.

So fierce were the Norse warriors that the kings of the Byzantine Empire kept some of them as their Varangian Guard to protect the royal household.

Though there were regional distinctions in language and culture, the modern nations of Denmark, Sweden and Norway would not exist for a few centuries yet to come. What the Norse shared more greatly outweighed their differences.

Though the Normans of Normandy conquered the land of Northern France, they adopted the language of the locals. Even so, they gave part of their own Scandinavian language to the locals. Later, when the Normans crossed the English Channel, they did the same—adopting the language of the locals, but adding to it their own Norman French, already flavored with its Norse influences.

Like their sagas and heroes, the Norse gods were also a rough and tumble group of individuals with strong character and human frailties.

This work on Norse mythology is divided into two main parts. The first will tackle the heroes, their sagas and history. In the second part of the book, we will peer into the heart of Norse religious myth.

Part 1—Heroes and Sagas

Twelve winters of grief for Hrothgar, king

Of the Danes, sorrow heaped at his door

By hell-forged hands, His misery leaped

The seas, was told and sung in all

Men's ears

—*Beowulf,* an English epic tale set in Scandinavia

Chapter 1—The Icelandic Sagas

Ingólfr looked back toward his wife and smiled. Soon, their voyage would be over. Soon, they would have a new home free from the threat of the blood feuds they had left behind in Noregi—their ancient homeland amongst the fjords of the North. Little Torstein looked up at him from behind his mother's skirt and admired his fearsome father—a man whose name meant "royal or kingly wolf."

With the fabled island of Garðar Svavarsson in sight, Ingólfr looked down at his high seat pillars—the icons of his status as chieftain—and nodded at the decision he had made the night before.

"Brother," he said to Hjörleifr Hróðmarsson, his step mother's son, "I have prayed to Odin to have his wisdom guide me. I swore an oath to him that if we should sight land, I will lay my pillars upon the sea for the gods to show me where I should build my settlement." He then waved to his brother to help him lift the pillars over the railing and they let them slide into the waters of the cold, north Atlantic.

The year was AD 871. The hardest years of deep cold were behind them. Before them lay the island Naddod had called "snow land," because it had started to sprinkle the white stuff before he had left several decades earlier. Naddod had missed his intended destination, the Faroe Islands, north of the Scots, and had been blown to the northwest. Later, Garðar had been on his way to the Hebrides, off the coast of Scotland, but also had been blown off course. He was the first to circumnavigate the island, confirming that indeed it was an island. That was only a decade earlier than now.

Finally, Ingólfr landed and his thralls and men set up camp. But it was to be a temporary camp. He had to wait for the gods to deliver his pillars to the coast of this island. Only then would he know where to build his new home.

For three years, two of his thralls—Vífill and Karli—searched the coastline, combing every mile time and again, searching for their chieftain's symbols of lordship. Finally, they found the pillars and Ingólfr had his location—a favorable bay on the southwestern coast of the island. There, he gave his settlement the name, Reykjavík, which meant "bay of smokes." The region was surrounded by many, natural, hot springs and the steam rising from them looked like smoke.

Later, Ingólfr found that his step-brother had been killed by his own men. He gave Hjörleifr a proper Norse funeral and then found his step-brother's men had escaped to Vestmannaeyjar (Westman Islands), just south of Iceland. There, the chieftain caught up with the murderers and slew them.

Ingólfr and his family had picked the right century to settle in Iceland. The far more temperate Medieval Warm Period was just starting. Nearly twenty-five percent of the island was covered by forests, so homebuilding would have plenty of resources. In our modern era, only one percent of the island has forests.

Ingólfr's slave, Karli, was not shy about criticizing his chieftain's settlement location. "How ill that we should pass good land, to settle in this remote peninsula."

Settlement continued for another sixty years, at the end of which, all of the arable land had been claimed.

Years later, with the death of his father, Torstein became the new chieftain and eventually founded the first *thing*—precursor to the Althingi, or national parliament. The Althingi was to become one of the longest running modern parliamentary bodies in the world.

Laws and Blood Feuds

In antiquity, the Norse handled disputes the old-fashioned way—with violence and bloodshed. Insults were numerous and the resulting violence was sometimes more numerous, because one act frequently led to many others in retaliation. One retaliation led to an explosion of counter-retaliations. Peace was sometimes only possible through extinction of one family, or through the realization that extinction was upon them.

To keep things from becoming too chaotic, certain laws were established so that blood feuds could be carried out with some sense of decorum. Perhaps we could call it "ordered chaos."

The Althing (Icelandic Alþingi) was first established AD 930 at Thingvellir (Þingvellir)—"Parliament fields" or "assembly fields." This open assembly was located about forty-five kilometers east of Ingólfr's settlement (now Reykjavík). The assembly was open to all free men. There, they would resolve disputes, hammer out new laws and even grant exceptions to existing laws.

In the days of the Vikings, the family was the key focus of society. If you hurt a free man, you also hurt his family. Blood feuds were common. But sometimes a wrongful death, even if accidental, did not necessarily have to result in violence and retribution. Sometimes the injured party or family could demand *weregild,* or blood money, as restitution. Every person and object of property was given a monetary value. Norwegian *gjeld* and Danish *gæld* meant "debt." The -*gäld* suffix in Swedish had a similar meaning—*gengäld* (exchange or in return), *återgälda* (return favor, retribute), and *vedergälda* (revenge). Of course, if the *weregild* was not paid, a blood feud would almost always ensue.

The madness of this cycle of retaliatory violence should seem obvious. Once started, there is no easy way to stop it, short of forgiveness. But this is not true forgiveness; this is merely a lull in the violence until one side or the other has a more clear advantage and the proper excuse to re-initiate the violence.

From this period of rugged survival and testy conflict, legends of heroes and struggle were born.

The Sagas

The Icelandic Sagas were tales of heroes and their families who settled in Iceland, and of their descendents. Some of the most popular sagas include, Grettis saga, Njáls saga, Egils saga, Laxdæla saga, Gísla saga, and Hrafnkels saga. The stories would include anecdotes of family life, tales of raiding parties to win booty and honor for their family, stories of conquest and even accounts of feuds between families.

In Egil's saga, for instance, the tale spans a century and a half of the family of Kveldulf ("evening wolf"), Egil's grandfather. Harold Fairhair wanted to become king of all Norway and it looked as though he might well accomplish this feat. He called upon Kveldulf to serve in his army, but Kveldulf was now an old man. The king asked for him to send one of his sons, instead, but he refused. Eventually, the strife between Kveldulf's family and that of Harold, would force Kveldulf's family to flee the country and to settle in the newly opened land of Iceland. The bulk of the saga is about Egil, a complex character full of seemingly whimsical violence and great skill at poetry. But when we dig deeper, we find that Egil holds in high regard such values as respect, honor, friendship and loyalty. His violence only comes when these are betrayed.

Egil's saga and several other writings were thought to be the work of Snorri Sturluson (1179–1241), twice voted lawspeaker of the Althingi. He posed the idea that the gods were, in truth, merely mortal men—kings and great heroes of the past who were venerated for generations until each was remembered merely as a divine being, rather than a skillful king.

A note on Icelandic names—most citizens of Iceland used a patronym, rather than a family name, a practice which continues even unto today. This means that the given name is followed by the given name of the person's father. Some surnames in English cultures were originally patronyms, like Peterson (Peter's son). The father's given name has a genitive suffix appended which merely means "son of" (-son) or "daughter of" (-dóttir). This is a holdover from the days of the Vikings when Leif Ericson—the first known European to visit mainland North America—truly was the son of Eric.

The Icelandic sagas were part of the inspiration for Jules Verne's science fiction story, *Journey to the Center of the Earth,* published 1864. The main character in that story, Professor Lindenbrock of Scotland, found an artifact which included an original saga by Snorri Sturluson. It told of an entrance to the center of our world.

Later, American writer, Edgar Rice Burroughs, was inspired by Verne's work and created his own story named, *Pellucidar,* first published 1915. The influence of the sagas has run deep in our culture.

In the next chapter, we look at Vikings in the decadent, imperial halls of Byzantium, where the Varangian Guard protected the royal household.

Chapter 2—The Varangian Guard

Bjørn Olavson trudged along the Dnieper River enjoying the fine spring day in eastern Europe. He had just left his cousins in Kiev. They worked for the Kievan Rus in helping to establish order after its conquest the year before by Helgi of Novgorod. Visiting them, he had learned of work in the Byzantine capital, Constantinople—or what the locals called *Vasileos Polis*—city of the emperor—or simply, *Polis* (The City).

Actually, Kiev had already belonged to the Norse. One of Rørik's men, Höskuldr, had conquered the city earlier, but Helgi grew outraged when the man became Baptized by the Christians, forsaking Odin, Thor and the other Norse gods.

And here, Bjørn was traveling to that more distant capital of corruption itself, run by Christians for more than 500 years. For all he had ever heard of that spiritual tradition, he wondered if the religion had also become corrupted, instead of it having corrupted the city, as some seemed to claim.

At nineteen years of age, his only real concern was finding good work. Back home, more than a century of cold climate and poor farming had driven a lot of people away. The Norsemen were taking new lands, as they had done in these regions north of the Black Sea. For all intents and purposes, Vikings ruled the rivers of Eastern Europe—the Dnieper, Dniester and Volga trade routes.

The year by Christian understanding was 883, and it was going to be a good year for Bjørn. In the *Polis,* Norsemen had been helping the emperor for nearly a decade. From what his cousins had told him, these flatulent, soft southerners couldn't keep their word any better than their gas. So, an honorable *víkingr,* such as himself, would have a strong advantage over his more malleable competition. Bjørn would never betray his word once given.

Up ahead, he could see a river boat boarding to head downriver and perhaps out to the Black Sea and beyond. It might take him all the way to the entrance of the Black Sea and to the imperial city itself.

Who Were These Varangians?

Most casual students of history may never have heard of the Varangian Guard. The image of Vikings protecting royalty in the Byzantine (Eastern Roman) Empire may seem too strange to believe. But it happened.

The word itself was the name given to them by the eastern Slavs and the Greeks of the Byzantine Empire. The Vikings adopted their term into their own language of Old Norse—*Væringjar*.

A Viking might steal from you, but if he were to give you his word, he would likely die before failing to live up to his oath. This was not perfect, by any means, but as a rule of thumb, it placed Vikings far above others in the category of trust. Thus, these fierce warriors were increasingly sought after, especially in corrupt Byzantium which saw alliances shift like quicksand. Despite being Christian, liars and betrayers were common in high places.

In fact, the Varangians were so popular, that places like southern Sweden were losing too many of their own, good fighting men. There, they passed a law forbidding inheritance to those who left to serve in "Greece"—what the Scandinavians called Byzantium or Constantinople (the Polis). But other European courts later came to demand Varangian warriors, too. Not surprisingly, the Kievan Rus recruited them, from about 980 to 1060. And the Anglo-Saxon court in London hired them, from about 1018 to 1066, when their cousins, the Normans conquered all of England at the Battle of Hastings.

The northern, Russian city of Novgorod (literally "new fortification," later "new city") was already a thriving town when it was conquered some time before or during 860 by Rørik (Rurik), one of the Varangian chieftains. "Conquered" may be too strong a word, because we don't know many details from that period. We know that Rørik made the city his capital, after he had been invited by some of the warring tribes of the region to reestablish order. It was one of the stopping points on the Varangian trading route from the Baltics (Scandinavia) to the Balkans (Greek domain).

Later, Rørik (830–879) sent Höskuldr (Askold) and some of his men to conquer Kiev, a city now in the modern nation of Ukraine. The Vikings were now taking over much of their own trade route. This not only helped to protect that trade route, but it also gave them more land in a milder climate than their own cold North. In 860, Höskuldr attacked Constantinople, but was repulsed by Emperor Michael III and his forces.

When Rørik died in 879, Helgi (Oleg of Novgorod), Höskuldr's brother, took Rørik's place as ruler of the Nordic Rus.

We have conflicting rumors about the demise of Höskuldr. One of them tells us that he became baptized as a Christian, perhaps to quell the restless natives he now managed for his boss and distant relative, Rørik. Höskuldr was said to have been the grandson of the legendary Ragnar Lodbrok.

When Helgi heard of this religious conversion, he took it upon himself to take Kiev from Höskuldr. The year was 882. We can only guess that Helgi (?–912) may have been outraged at Höskuldr's betrayal of the old ways. Some historians feel that Helgi merely tricked his brother, then killed him, and that it may have had nothing to do with religious conversion and more to do with greed.

Helgi established the Kievan Rus and ruled over it until 912. The name, "Russia," comes from the Nordic Rus.

It may seem ironic for businessmen, albeit also warriors, to attack their largest customer. But some of the Varangian attacks on Constantinople resulted in favorable trade agreements for the Kievan Rus. The year 907 included one of those attacks from Helgi, the leader of Kiev. As a result, Emperor Leo VI tried to pay off Helgi. The payment wasn't enough. The Rus attacked again in 911 and Leo VI finally gave Helgi the trade deal he sought. In exchange, Helgi offered some of his own, fierce Varangian warriors. Historical records, dated 911, show that a sizable group of Varangians fought as Byzantine mercenaries.

The Byzantine Empire had been the successor state of the Roman Empire, and before it, the Roman Republic. For more than 1,500 years these people had ruled a large chunk of Eurasia, but their world would barely last another 600 years. Byzantium was corrupt, with politicians buying favors, powerful psychopaths murdering their way to the top and local-born guards being bought out cheap to betray their masters.

Though the Byzantine government had made use of Varangian warriors as far back as 874, it wasn't until 988 that the Varangians were officially made the imperial guard. How that came about proves to be its own interesting story.

Prince Vladimir I of Kiev had taken the Empire's chief base in the Crimea—Chersonesos. Emperor Basil II was outraged, but he negotiated with the fierce barbarians. Vladimir agreed to vacate Chersonesos and even to supply Basil with 6,000 of his own Varangian warriors. In exchange, he wanted to marry Anna (963–1011), Basil's younger sister.

Basil didn't like the idea. The thought of his refined sister marrying a heathen from the North was repulsive in the very least. Anna wasn't too keen about the idea, either. Ultimately, Vladimir was able to sweeten the deal by agreeing to be baptized and to have his own people convert to Christianity. The royal couple were wed in 989, in the pleasant Crimea. Vladimir was 31; Anna was 26.

The marriage legitimized the Kievan Rus in a way that sheer strength and cunning could not. In the high society of the 10th and 11th centuries, Byzantine royalty rubbed off on Kiev, and hundreds of years later, the Grand Duchy of Moscow could logically lay claim to the title, "The Third Rome." After all, the power of the Roman Empire went to Constantinople when Rome fell in the 5th century. And with Byzantium gone, centuries later, Russia then had some of that royal blood flowing in its veins.

Vladimir and Anna may not have lived happily ever after, but they were well guarded by the Varangian warriors Vladimir had kept for himself.

In the next chapter, we take a brief look at Vikings in America.

Chapter 3—Vikings in America

I remember the shock when I learned that Christopher Columbus wasn't the first European to "discover" America. But the notion of anyone discovering a place where people already lived is a bit weak, at best. I mean, come on! The original inhabitants of the Americas came from Asia and elsewhere. They were the "first," as far as we know. And that's a key concept in science and in history—"as far as we know." We can always discover more evidence later that blows our original ideas out of the proverbial water. Some controversial evidence found in Brazil suggests that the Phoenicians may have visited the

Americas hundreds of years earlier than the confirmed "first" Europeans.

So, who beat Chris Columbus? The Vikings, that's who. Columbus made his tropical discovery in 1492. Erik the Red discovered his icy new home in about 980—more than five centuries earlier. Later, Erik's son, Leif, explored mainland America.

Erik Thorvaldsson (c.950–c.1003) was born in Rogaland, Norway, Jæren district. However, his father, Thorvald Asvaldsson, had killed a man and was banished from his homeland. Thorvald moved his family to Iceland. There, young Eric—called "the Red" because of his red hair and beard—eventually set up a farm and married a local girl named Thjodhild. Everything seemed to be going well in his life until word came to him that two of his thralls had been killed.

"Master!" said Hallvard, running in from the field.

"What is it?" asked Erik. He grew annoyed that his thrall was still catching his breath.

"Your other," the slave panted, then continued, "two of your thralls. Killed. Eyiolf the Foul, master."

"Why?" asked Erik. "What right?" He put down the implement he had been fixing and waved for Hallvard to lead the way. "Where?"

"Valthjof's farm. They started a landslide and Valthjof got angry. He told his friend, Eyiolf, and he slew your thralls."

"Damn it!" said Erik. "I needed those men here on the farm."

It took a little more than twenty minutes for the master to stride across his own land and that of his neighbor to reach his house.

"Valthjof!" Erik called out as he approached. "What is the meaning of this?"

"You! What are you doing on my land?"

"So, where is your friend, Eyiolf?"

Valthjof came out of his house, followed by Eyiolf and Holmgang-Hrafn. "He's here. We had our right to kill your thralls. They were doing some foolishness on the hill next to my land and caused a landslide that destroyed my fence and killed one of my cattle."

"You fool!" shouted Erik. "And you didn't take the time to talk to me? To ask for compensation? I needed those men."

Eyiolf laughed. "You should teach your thralls to be more careful. Your idiots weren't worth keeping in any event. I actually did you a service. Perhaps, you're too dumb to know the difference between a smart thrall and a dumb one."

Erik's face turned red at the insult, almost as red as his hair. Then, he realized that he still had the hammer in his hand. One powerful swing and the hammer found its way into Eyiolf's head, crushing his skull. The man crumpled to the ground.

Valthjof turned and ran, but Holmgang-Hrafn started to draw his sword. Erik closed the distance before the man could free his blade. Again, the hammer found skull bone and made it soft with his powerful swing.

For nearly a minute, Erik stood there over the body, looking at it, blinking and scowling at the crumpled form of the man. Then, he nodded once, turned and waved to Hallvard. "Back to Eiríksstadir."

As Erik returned to his home, his mind was seething with dark thoughts. Surely, this would not end well.

Nearing his house, he called out, "Thjodhild! Get our children. Go to Thorgest. Stay there with him and his wife until I get things settled. I have killed two men at Valthjof's place. Go!"

After his wife had grabbed a few things, their teenage sons, young daughter and left, Erik went back to work on his farm, settling into his chores until someone came to make their complaint.

The next day, most of the men of Haukadal came to pay him a visit. Eyiolf's kinsmen demanded that Erik be banished for the murder.

"And Eyiolf?" asked Erik. "He murdered my thralls. I needed those men for my farm."

"But they're only thralls," said Gunnbjörn. "You killed a free man. Actually, two."

"Yes, and the second was pulling his sword. I would've been happy to have left him alone, had he not threatened me with deadly force."

The elder sucked on his lower lip for a few moments, squinted, and said, "We don't want you here."

"Thor's hammer! Fine," said Erik. "When people like you dismiss crimes of others, but condemn those of mine, I want no part of you, either. You invite injustice with your dishonor."

After his visitors had left, Erik went to retrieve his wife and son from Thorgest. Before he left his friend's place, he had a favor to ask.

"Thorgest," said Erik, "I've been banished from Haukadal. The Hawk's Dale will not see me again, unless... I must ask a favor. We need to travel light. Could you hold my *setstokkr* until I come to retrieve them?"

He was talking about the sacred ornamental beams his father had brought from Norway. The Vikings were a superstitious lot. To them, such trappings for their homes were considered to be of important, mystical value.

"Yes, my friend. I will do that for you. I am sorry that this has ended this way for you."

"Me, too, my friend. It shouldn't take more than a few weeks for me to build a new house. I'll be back then."

Time passed quickly. Erik moved his family to Öxney Island, northeast of Snæfellsnes Peninsula, at the entrance to Hrammsfjördhur, one of the key fjörds of Western Iceland. Starting over was something his family was getting used to.

But when he returned to Haukadal to retrieve his *setstokkr* from Thorgest, the man did not have good news.

"But I received your word that you would hold them for me. Where are they?" demanded Erik.

"I don't know what you mean," replied Thorgest. "I don't have your *setstokkr*. You are mistaken. Now, leave. You're upsetting my family. After all, you've been banished from this vale. You shouldn't even be here."

Erik could not believe he was hearing this from someone he thought was his friend. He hid his feelings and left. How could a Viking break his oath?

The next day, when Thorgest had left his farm for supplies, Erik returned with his remaining thralls and took the *setstokkr* from the man's own home. As they were leaving, Thorgest's wife saw them.

Before Erik could make it back to the ship, Thorgest, his two sons and several other men had caught up with him.

"So, you're a thief and a murderer," said Thorgest.

"And you are a dishonest and dishonorable liar," said Erik, "breaking your oath to me to hold my own *setstokkr* safe until my return." He nodded to his thralls to set the posts down.

Thorgest winced at the accusation, but didn't reply.

"See?" said Erik, turning to the other men standing with Thorgest. "He doesn't protest the truth. He promised to keep my *setstokkr* until my return. I thought we Norsemen valued our honor above life itself. And now he conveniently forgets his promise and won't tell me where he hid them. Or did he sell them? Did his dishonor stoop that low?"

"These are mine," said Thorgest. "They've been in my family for more than three hundred years."

"They're mine, now," said Erik. "You forfeited your right to them by your deceit."

At that, one of Thorgest's sons lunged at Erik with his sword. Tired even before the fighting had begun, Erik was nonetheless prepared. His dagger found the young man's stomach and the son keeled over in agony. Finally, Erik drew his own sword and tossed his knife to one of his thralls—the one with known fighting experience.

When the melee had run its course, both of Thorgest's sons and several other men lay dead. Erik and his thralls were unharmed.

An assembly was called and Erik was again banished, but this time for three years from all of Iceland.

"These people have been dishonorable," said Erik to his wife. He shook his head and motioned for their two sons and her, holding their daughter, to board their ship.

The year was 982, and the Norse had lived in Iceland for a century. This was Erik's second home. Now, the fates were sending him out to his death, or to some third home, as yet unknown.

He had heard the tales of Gunnbjörn Ulfsson and Snæbjörn Galti. Both had seen an island to the West. Gunnbjörn had sighted the land more than half a century earlier, but had never landed. He had been blown off course and had been anxious to return home to Iceland. Four years before today, Snæbjörn had taken Gunnbjörn's story to heart and had attempted to sail there, but his men had revolted, resulting in Snæbjörn's death.

Finally, good fortune was smiling on Erik the Red. His voyage went relatively smoothly. He rounded Cape Farewell at the southern tip of the island, and explored the western coast until he found viable land comparable to that he had left in Iceland. When finally his three years of exile were up, he returned to Iceland in order to sell others on the notion of settling those new lands. The thought of returning to Iceland with its faithless neighbors did not sit well with him, but he was certain he could find honorable folk willing to build a new home for themselves.

"People would be attracted to go there if it had a favorable name," he told his wife. "I shall call it Greenland. That's far better than the name, 'Iceland'."

After spending the winter in Iceland, he returned to Greenland with twenty-five ships full of settlers. The seas were rough, however, and eleven of them did not make it.

Good Timing and Eric's Destiny

At times during this age of Viking settlements, the rate of warming was faster than at any decade during the 20th century. The world was coming out of another period of cold climate—the second coldest during the Holocene interglacial of the current Ice Age. But the deepest cold lasted no more than a century or two. In a little over two centuries, Earth went from the coldest in recent memory to another warm period peak. This was the Medieval Warm Period and Greenland had become far more hospitable than it ever was in modern times.

The Roman Warm Period, a thousand years earlier, had been significantly warmer. Likewise, the Minoan Warm Period, a thousand years before that, was even warmer. Though Eric the Red lived through the second coldest warm period of the Holocene, at least he had its beneficial warmth. Their survival depended on a milder northern climate, and Greenland, unlike

Norway, had little benefit from the Gulf Stream's tropical warmth.

Erik's small settlement eventually grew to two settlements and a total of 5,000 people with nearly 400 farms later discovered by archaeologists.

The Vikings had made contact with the natives, who they called "Skræling"—what Columbus later would have called "Indian."

The settlements on Greenland lasted from 985 to some time in the 14th or 15th century. The Western Settlement was abandoned about 1350. Greenland's Eastern Settlement was tested by radiocarbon dating and the youngest man-made materials there were from about 1430.

One key reason for the decline of Erik's legacy was the end of the Medieval Warm Period and the start of the Little Ice Age, traditionally dated at 1350.

Erik's destiny had given his people a new home that had lasted nearly 500 years.

Leif Erikson's Destiny

Leif was Erik's second son. At 29, Leif had sailed back to Norway (AD 999) and had, during his stay, become part of the household guard of King Olaf Tryggvason.

The Norwegians converted Leif to Christianity and commissioned him to spread the word of Christ to the folk back in Greenland. At 31, he returned to his home (AD 1001) and kept his promise. His mother, Thjodhild, readily accepted the teachings and even arranged for the building of the first church there. But his father, Erik, rejected the teachings, preferring to keep the old ways of the Norse gods—Odin, Thor and the others.

The history of Leif's discoveries remain unclear; there are conflicting stories. One says that he discovered the American mainland by accident. Another states that he had merely heard of an earlier sighting by one of the original settlers whose ship had been blown off course. Here, we will follow the latter of these stories.

Seventeen years earlier, in 985, Bjarni Herjólfsson had been on that lost ship. Eleven other ships had been destroyed in a storm that blew his ship off course. He sighted land to the West, but he knew that his destination had been bypassed to the East. Anxious to arrive at his father's farm, Bjarni ignored the land he had sighted and headed for Greenland.

Leif had heard of this new land from Bjarni and, in the year 1002, even bought Bjarni's ship in order to make the voyage. Moreover, Leif talked his father into joining the expedition, but Erik fell off his horse as he had neared the ship. Taking this as a bad omen, he had decided to stay behind. That decision would ultimately kill him, because a recently landed group of immigrants from Iceland had carried with them an epidemic which would decimate the settlement, killing many of its inhabitants, including Erik the Red. Had he gone with his son, he would likely have survived.

After gathering a crew of thirty-five men, Leif used Bjarni's path in reverse, heading west to Baffin Island, which he called Helluland (meaning Flat Rock Land), and then south to Labrador, which he called Markland (meaning Forest Land). This last landing drew the interest of everyone aboard, because Greenland did not have forests. The lumber would be a much needed resource.

Two more days of sailing southward landed them at Newfoundland Island, in what is today, Eastern Canada. Leif called it "Vinland," because the men he had tasked with exploring the land found wild grapes growing there. Today, at the northern end of that island, there is a national historic site named, L'Anse aux Meadows, which commemorates the landing of Leif Erikson and his men.

The name Vinland has remained controversial, especially its location. Because Massachusetts is the farthest north that grapes currently grow on the Atlantic coast, some researchers claimed that "Vinland" had to be farther south.

The scientists who excavated L'Anse aux Meadows suggested that "Vinland" did not mean "wine land," but "land of meadows." What both groups of scientists forget is that climate always changes. The period around AD 1000 was far warmer than today and it remains quite possible that grapes grew as far north as L'Anse aux Meadows. During the same period, wine grapes also grew in Northern England where today it is impossible to grow them, because it is now so much colder. It remains ironic that the news talks so often about "warmest year on record," when we have evidence of so many far warmer years in this ongoing Ice Age.

Winter was closing in, so Leif decided to wait until spring before returning to Greenland. There was plenty of salmon, so they knew they would have sufficient food. Plus, they had the grapes his men had discovered. When winter was over, Leif and his men went back home, carrying with them a load of timber and grapes.

On the way, Leif rescued an Icelandic sailor and crew who had become shipwrecked. For that, Leif Erikson earned "Leif the Lucky" as his nickname.

Leif's older brother, Thorvald also made a trip to Vinland, but the gruff Norsemen didn't know how to deal with the skittish nature of the Skraelings—the natives of the land. After a misunderstanding that escalated into deadly conflict, Thorvald was killed by a native's arrow. His crew escaped and returned to Greenland.

When Thorstein heard that his older brother had died, he made preparations to go to Vinland in order to retrieve Thorvald's body. He and his wife, Gudrid, started the voyage, but were turned back by rough seas. They ended up spending the winter at another settlement in Greenland. During the cold season, an epidemic took Gudrid's husband and several others. The painful irony was that Thorstein was her second husband. Her first had also died of illness after having arrived in Greenland.

But Gudrid would not remain lonely for long. An Icelandic merchant named, Thorfinn Karlsefni Thórdarson, fell in love with Gudrid and married her.

Thorfinn has long been known simply as Thorfinn Karlsefni—the second part of his name meaning "real man," "a thorough man," "sterling man," or "makings of a man."

Despite all his manliness, he could not say "no" when Gudrid coaxed him to move to Vinland. Leif liked the idea that someone else was interested in the part-time settlement he had started there, but he was only willing to lend the houses he had built in Vinland. He would not make a free gift of any of them.

While Thorfinn's family lived in Vinland, Gudrid bore him a son named Snorri. So great was Thorfinn's nickname that his son, Snorri Thorfinnson was sometimes called Snorri Karlsefnisson. He was the first known European to have been born in the Americas, outside of Greenland. He would later return to Iceland and would become instrumental in the conversion of that island nation to Christianity. Many modern Icelanders can trace their roots back to Snorri Karlsefnisson.

Visitors to Vinland called Leif's camp, *Leifsbúðir* (meaning Leif's booths). But because of the continuing problems with the natives, the settlement was short-lived. Throughout most of its history, it acted as temporary shelter for supply runs and trading expeditions.

Thorfinn Karlsefni—In Modern Art and Fiction

In Philadelphia, Pennsylvania, United States, a statue of Thorfinn Karlsefni was erected on Kelly Drive and unveiled in late 1920. The benefactor who financed the sculpture and its installation wanted to preserve this piece of American history.

The Japanese manga (cartoon), *Vinland Saga,* started in 2005, is based loosely on the life of Thorfinn Karlsefni.

The science fiction novel, *Touch the Stars: Emergence,* by John Dalmas and Carl Martin uses *Thorfinn Karlsefni* as the name of an interstellar ship of exploration, visiting first Alpha Centauri's fictional planet, Veopul. In the sequel by Carl Martin, *Touch the Stars: Diaspora,* the Karlsefni continues its exploration of other star systems, with the owner's son, Gordon Roanhorse, as its cabin boy and junior officer in-training.

In the next chapter, we turn our sights to the warmer climate of the Mediterranean and Sicily. Yes, the Vikings were there, too.

Chapter 4—The Vikings of Sicily

Unlike the Norman conquest of England, the Norse conquest of Sicily was messy and took many decades, many battles and many generals.

At first, the Normans of the Mediterranean were mercenaries working for either the Lombards of northern Italy (centered on Genoa), or the Byzantine forces of the Empire (centered on Constantinople).

In AD 999, the Byzantine Empire ruled portions of what is today southern Italy. The Byzantines had ruled over Sicily from 535 to 965, after taking it away from the Germanic tribes who had taken the island from the Romans. From 827 to 965, systematic attacks by the

Muslims ultimately took the island from the Empire. Muslim attacks on the Italian mainland threatened to expand their territory. In 999, the Norman Vikings started to appear on the battlefield. This was only ten years after Vladimir I of Kiev had married the Emperor's sister, Anna. The Emperor had his Varangian Guard to protect him, and plenty of extra Viking warriors to throw into battle.

When the Viking mercenaries won their battles, sometimes they kept the territory for themselves. This left the Lombards and the Byzantines shaking their heads.

Some seventy years after the Byzantines had lost Sicily to the Arabs, Byzantine general George Maniakes led Varangian and Norman mercenaries into Sicily in an attempt to take back the island (1038).

In 1057, Roger of Hauteville arrived in southern Italy. He was the youngest son of Tancred of Hauteville, Normandy and his second wife. Already, his older brother William (c1009–1046) had started the conquest of southern Italy. Roger was also ambitious. He and his brother, Robert Guiscard finished the conquest of Calabria and Apulia, and then turned their sights on Sicily. In May 1061, they took Messina. By 1072, they had taken Palermo. Syracuse fell in 1086, and they finished taking the entire island by 1091. Though Roger died in 1101, his son, Roger II, by his third wife, would go on to become the King of Sicily.

The Hauteville rule over Sicily would somewhat end with Roger II's grandson, William II, because he had no children. Why "somewhat?" Roger II's daughter, Constance, had married Henry VI, the Holy Roman Emperor. At her request, he snatched Sicily from ruin and chaos. So, in a very real sense, the Kingdom of Sicily stayed in the family, though ruled by a German king.

In the next chapter, we take a look at some of the background behind the Norman conquest of England— a story that is rarely told in any detail in the history books.

Chapter 5—Norman Conquest of England

Most schoolbook treatments of the Norman conquest of England focus on William the Conqueror and barely mention King Harald Hardrada of Norway, if at all. In many ways, Harald was the last of the Vikings. After his reign, things in the northlands became progressively more civilized, if you can call dozens of wars and other violence, "civilized." But after his time, the days of Viking raids and berserkers was coming to an end.

Already, the strength of character that had made Karlsefni a "real man," and had kept the Varangian

Guard honorable enough to keep their oath to the Byzantine Emperor, had established the ruling class in at least four non-Nordic countries:

- Norman France
- England
- Russia
- Sicily

Through marriage, this list would likely be significantly larger. For one, we saw how Constance, daughter of King Roger II of Sicily, became Queen of the Holy Roman Empire. These barbarians were moving up in the world. Their ruthless take on life molded the world around them through alliances and, at times, brute force.

Harald Sigurdsson (c.1015–1066) earned the nickname "Hardrada," which meant "harsh ruler," or "stern counsel." The reason may stem from his need to fight his way to the top.

At the tender age of fifteen (1030), he fought alongside Olaf Haraldsson, his half-brother, who had wanted to reclaim the throne he had lost to Danish King Cnut the Great in 1028. But let us be clear; in the days of Vikings, Norsemen were almost never tender at fifteen. Viking boys became men at, or shortly after puberty. Some were even kings in their mid-teens.

Harald and Olaf survived, despite their defeat by Cnut's loyal forces. But this left Harald in exile. He made his way south to the Kievan Rus, where he was eventually commissioned as Captain by Grand Prince Yaroslav the Wise. The prince's wife, Ingegerd, was a distant relative, so Harald was well-received at court. For the next few years, Harald built his skills and his following.

Feeling restless, Harald left Kiev in 1034, with about 500 men he had commanded. They joined the Varangian Guard in Constantinople, the city which they called Miklagard.

Though the Varangian Guard, by this time, was primarily for the protection of the Emperor and his household, Harald spent a great deal of his time away from the capital. First, he led his men against Arab pirates. After subduing the pirates on the seas, Harald turned to quelling the lines of pirate support found in the interior towns of Asia Minor.

By 1035, when the Byzantine forces had pushed all Arab influence out of what is today the modern nation of Turkey, Harald had become the commander of all the Varangians. Later, Harald fought in Jerusalem, and in 1038, Harald's forces joined those of General George Maniakes's campaign to recapture Sicily from the Saracens, for the Byzantine Empire. Though the campaign was initially successful, another Norman group and the Lombards revolted, and the once strong alliance fell apart. Soon, Harald's Varangians were fighting against William of Hauteville—older brother of Roger I, and uncle to future King Roger II of Sicily. Norman cousin was fighting Norman cousin.

In 1041, Harald's forces were sent to quell the Bulgarian uprising, where he earned the nickname "Bulgar burner." Though Emperor Michael IV heaped great honors on Harald, the Norwegian royal would soon lose favor in the Byzantine court. Later that same year, in December, the Emperor was dead from a prolonged illness.

The new emperor put Harald in prison. There are conflicting accounts as to why he was imprisoned and also how he escaped. But escape he did, returning to Kievan Rus. While a member of the Varangian Guard, Harald had amassed a great fortune. Naturally, wanting to secure that fortune for his own, future use, he sent it to Grand Prince Yaroslav for safekeeping.

There, in 1042, Harald married Ellisif (Elizabeth), Yaraslav's daughter, reclaimed his fortune and then helped Yaroslav's campaign to attack Constantinople. And why not? The new emperor had put him in prison. And even though that new emperor had been deposed and blinded, Harald now felt no loyalty to the corrupt regime that had betrayed him.

Three years later (1045), Harald grew homesick for Norway and anxious to reclaim the throne that should have been his half-brother's. But Olaf had died 15 years earlier. Legally, the throne should have been his. Some scholars think that Harald felt the need to return home because he had learned that the Norwegian crown had been returned to his family, but to an illegitimate son of Olaf—Magnus the Good. Not only that, Magnus was also king of Denmark. The irony likely acted as an insult to Harald who had suffered at age fifteen to the humiliation of losing his first major battle to the followers of King Cnut of Denmark. Now, an illegitimate had both crowns!

Harald contacted Magnus's competition in Denmark, Sweyn Estridsson, and also the Swedish king, Anund Jacob. Their combined forces attacked Denmark, hoping to draw Magnus away from Norway. But Magnus's advisors recommended not fighting his uncle

Harald. Magnus was in dire need of funds and Harald was rich. They agreed that Magnus would share the rule over Norway in exchange for Harald sharing his riches, but Magnus would hold the superior position. Though each co-regent held separate courts, they did occasionally meet. Those meetings almost always ended poorly with strong words and threats of violence.

In 1047, after two years of uneasy joint rule, Magnus died at the age of twenty-three. Magnus had made it clear that Harald would take Norway and Sweyn would take Denmark, if he should die. Harald, however, had grander ideas. He liked the idea of a unified, "North Sea Empire." He wanted what Cnut had possessed for a short while. But try as he might, he could not conquer Denmark.

With all of his scheming, Harald needed to pay more attention to holding onto what he had at home in Norway. Not everyone thought he made the best king and Harald needed to build alliances amongst the Norwegian aristocracy. King Harald had been a valiant warrior and commander, but as a negotiator and diplomat, he was a "hard ruler" to deal with. And this is where he earned the Hardrada nickname.

To make headway in the realm of aristocracy, Harald decided to seek out the most powerful families of Norway. To seal the bond, he married Tora Torbergsdatter, from one of those influential houses. Thus, Harald established for himself quite a dynasty. His children by Ellisif included Ingegerd, the future queen of Denmark and Sweden, and by Tora, Magnus II, King of Norway, and Olaf III, King of Norway.

Quite often, Harald took to the seas to explore the boundaries of his own realm, perhaps making his way to Spitsbergen and Novaya Zemlya. He may even have heard of Vinland, and may even have considered the lengthy task to visit that distant outpost. If he did consider a visit, the thought likely didn't last long. A perpetual war with Denmark kept him busy close to home. And at home, Harald spent far too much time brutalizing his own subjects. Harald was a villain to his own people, burning farms, plus maiming and killing those who showed any resistance to his policies. These acts, too, likely added to the nickname he had earned.

After multiple efforts to conquer Denmark, Harald finally agreed to a truce in 1065.

England had been ruled by Harthacnut, Cnut the Great's son. But Harthacnut had died in 1042 without a successor. A pact between Magnus the Good and Harthacnut stated that whoever died first, the other would take their title. Magnus, however, had been unable to make any claim to England stick. In the meantime, Englishman Edward the Confessor had stepped in to claim the throne. In 1045, Magnus had started toward England to reestablish his claim, but Sweyn Estridsson had started an uprising in Denmark. So, Magnus had needed to put his English aspirations on hold. To make matters worse, his uncle Harald had complicated things by joining Sweyn and the Swedish king against him.

Edward viewed the death of Magnus in 1047 as a reprieve. There were no clear threats to his crown at that time. To keep the possible threats at bay, Edward contacted his three most likely enemies and convinced them that each of them would be his successor. They were, King Harald, of course, but also King Sweyn of Denmark, and William of Normandy. Sweyn had been one of Magnus's successors, so may have had just as much right to England as did Harald. William of Normandy, however, was far closer—and William may well have been a distant relative of both Sweyn and

Harald. After all, the Normans had come from Scandinavia. Viking blood also ran in their veins.

Harald had already tested his forces against those of Edward, and knew that maintaining two simultaneous wars would not work. When he declared peace with Denmark, in 1065, he was then free to turn his attention to England.

When Edward died in early 1066, Harald was naturally upset that Harold Godwinson had been made king, instead. Godwinson had been only the son of one of Edward's advisors—not a strongly supported qualification. An advisor's son made king? Harold Godwinson was also Edward's brother-in-law, but that didn't make the Norwegian king feel any better.

Harold Godwinson had made an enemy of his brother, Tostig. After Harold G. had been made king, Tostig met with King Harald Hardrada and offered his services in helping the Norwegian king take over England, as Cnut's son had promised.

In August 1066, Harald left Norway with his wife, Ellisif, his son Olaf and his daughters. He left behind his wife Tora and made certain that his eldest son, Magnus would be made king should anything happen to him. He made his way to the Shetland Islands and then to Orkney, both already Norwegian territory.

There, he increased his forces with more soldiers, backed by several chieftains and lords. Next, he met with Tostig's ally, Malcolm III of Scotland, at Dunfermline. This added two thousand Scottish warriors.

In the meantime, Tostig left his home in exile and attacked from the South with his 12 ships filled with soldiers. He made his way north to meet with Harald's forces.

Harold Godwinson stayed in the South of England to ward off an attack expected from William of Normandy who had publicly claimed the throne of England for himself.

In September, King Harald Hardrada landed his forces in northern England amounting to nearly 300 longships and as much as 15,000 men. His was a far larger force than that of Tostig. They moved through Cleveland County toward a more populated region, plundering the coastal areas southward. The fighting started in earnest at Scarborough, Northern Yorkshire, where they met their first significant resistance. When Harald took to burning down the town, the other towns of Northumbria decided to surrender instead of losing everything. Other English forces moved in to stop the invasion and met Harald's forces at Fulford on September 20. The invaders won easily. And the city of York surrendered on September 24.

Harold Godwinson had heard of the invasion and arrived in York with his forces on the following day. He had traveled hard from the south of England, perhaps as long as nine days in transit.

The Norwegian king had expected to talk with the citizens of York to discuss the terms of surrender, but to his surprise, he met King Godwinson's forces at Stamford Bridge.

Harald Hardrada was, for once in his life, unprepared. He was not wearing his heavy, battle armor. And he was outnumbered, having left a good third of his forces with his longboats in Riccal, a few kilometers away.

Early in the battle, Harald, in the trance-like state of a berserker, was struck in the throat with an arrow and he died. The northern invaders lost. But Harold Godwinson had left his southern approach open for William of Normandy. And after nine days of forced march, plus a hard battle against the Norwegians and his disgruntled brother, Tostig, his forces were now exhausted.

Three days later—long before Harold Godwinson could return to the South—William's forces landed in Sussex, in the South of England.

On October 14, 1066, William's forces finally met those of Harold Godwinson. The Norman forces were far more clever on the battlefield and handily won the day. But William would not find peace for several years. English revolts were numerous and William's forces were kept busy putting down the succession of rebellions.

In 1070, even King Sweyn thought he might get lucky in England, but William paid him off. By 1072, peace had finally come to England.

Because of Harald Hardrada, William the Conqueror had an easier time of it defeating Harold Godwinson at the Battle of Hastings. Because Harald had attacked in the North, Godwinson had abandoned the South and had left it open for William's entrance.

Harald of Norway was an heroic figure, but also a bit of a psychopath. He took selfishness to a higher level, like all conquerors tend to do. He was fearless in his murder of others, but the world was a harsh place. In his world and time, you were either a victim or a perpetrator. Harald had decided to be a perpetrator for as long as he could.

In the next chapter, we take a brief look at the phenomenon known as "berserker."

Chapter 6—Berserkers

Legend tells of Viking warriors going into battle in a trance-like state as if on drugs or drunk with liquor. The English word "berserk" (crazy, out of control) comes from this phenomenon.

These fierce warriors from the North seemed fearless to an extreme. We can admire them for that. Philosopher Rod Martin, Jr. commented on the state we call "hero," remarking that a true hero is someone who has no concern for self. We admire the selflessness. But the Vikings were a conflicted lot. Sometimes they were self-concerned—especially when it came to greed (taking things from others), or ego (reacting to insults or harm to one's own group). In these, the Vikings were not so heroic. These tarnished traits showed their frailties—their weaknesses.

When the Viking warriors went berserk, they were an inspiration, despite their violence. They went into battle without armor or shields. They relied purely on cunning, skill and that elevated state some athletes occasionally reach when everything simply falls into place—a state they call "the zone."

In the Northlands, Viking warriors sometimes relied on the power of certain totems or animal spirits. One group relied on the bear and, during battle, would wear a coat or shirt *(serkr)* made from bear skin. Bears, it was thought, represented Odin—king of the Norse gods. To wear the bear skin was to gain the strength of a bear and also Odin's favor. Going "berserk" was a kind of shape-shifting—changing form *(hamask)*. Berserkers were the "bear shirts"—the bear warriors.

Another group took the wolf as their source of energy and battle savvy. These wolf warriors were called *Ulfhednar*. Wolf skins were their preferred dress for the battlefield. They also went berserk in battle—or "mad as hounds."

A third group relied on the wild boar for their inspiration. These boar warriors would lead the charge in what was called the *Svinfylking,* or boar's head. The Vanir gods of Norse mythology held the wild boar as a sacred beast. For instance, Freyr owned the giant boar, Gullinbursti, while his sister, the goddess Freyja owned the Hildisvíni—magical battle swine.

It was said that neither fire nor iron could touch these Berserkers, Ulfhednar and Svinfylking. So deep was their passion that the berserker could not tell friend from foe, so their fellow warriors knew to keep their distance.

When the Vikings crossed the North Sea to invade England or France, they traveled in their longboats which frequently had prows of dragon heads. From where did the inspiration come to fashion their ship prows as dragons? Researcher, Rod Martin, Jr. suggests that there may have been dragons at some time in the past, but that they were not living, breathing animals as they are in the modern fantasies. The odd stories of dragons from around the world can more easily be explained as the primitive's perception of man-made aircraft which used a technology still unknown to our modern science. Thus, the tale of Cadmus fighting his golden dragon and the sudden appearance of soldiers can be explained as a dragon airship and its warrior passengers. The tale of Cecrops, supposedly half-man, half-snake, can be explained simply as the dragon airship's captain popping his hatch to talk to his men on the outside. And the tale of Medea flying away from Athens on a golden dragon was merely the same dragon airship which had protected the Golden Fleece back home in Colchis. The ancestors of these berserkers may well have known a dragon airship or two, and the powerful image of those ships had left a lasting impression on their culture.

In Part 2, we delve into the world of the gods.

Part 2—The Norse Gods

"It is better to stand and fight. If you run, you'll only die tired."

—A Viking saying

Chapter 7— Vanir against the Aesir

In Norse mythology, there were two main groups of gods. The Vanir were like the rustic, Nordic folk who first arrived at the foot of the ice mountains before they melted from the face of northern Europe. The Aesir were like the urban barbarians who built towns and longships.

The Vanir were the folk of Utangard—"beyond the protection of the fence." The Aesir were the folk of Innangard—"within the protection of the fence." Even the names of their realms speak of this difference.

The Vanir were from Vanaheim, while the Aesir were from Asgard. The -gard suffix took on the connotation of fortified places full of laws and order. Even the realm of the humans fell within this protection, for they lived in Midgard. The Vanir, on the other hand, were from that chaotic realm that was both ancient and wild.

Freya's Magic

One of the Vanir goddesses, named Freya, had a special talent for changing destiny. To earn her keep, she went from town to town selling her "art of seidr." When finally she had made her way to Asgard, she was going by the name Heidr, which meant "bright." The powerful Aesir gods appreciated her talents perhaps more than they should. Calling upon Freya to change their fate became a fanatical fad, in some ways like a powerful street drug. The ease of instant gratification is somewhat similar these days to the corruption of our modern youth with fast food diseases and internet theft to guide their morals into darkness. The gods of Asgard were giving up their honor in order to satisfy their basest desires. No longer did they uphold obedience, honor and kin loyalty. They replaced these with a lust for more of Freya's powerful magic.

dispersed. The Aesir who lingered had wanted to make certain she was gone. The Vanir had hoped for some last moment reprieve, but found no solace in the result.

When most everyone had left, a few of the Vanir servants came to clean up the ashes, but found the pile moving. With increasing speed, the mound of ash grew, and grew, then suddenly rose up and cast off the debris, revealing the naked form of Freya. Her laughter echoed throughout the halls of Asgard and all of the Aesir came running back to find out what had happened.

Again, they bound her. Again, they placed kindling at her feet. And again, they lit the kindling in order to destroy the witch once and for all. This time, they did it more out of fear than blind arrogance.

And again, Freya rose up from the ashes, like the phoenix from Greek legend.

A third time, they bound her, and lit the flame in a near panic of desperation. Only Odin kept any semblance of cool resolve. Not once did he see the error of his criminal act. He was too blinded with the arrogance of his own self-righteousness.

Like most of the gods of the ancient world, the Aesir were sometimes a cruel and irresponsible lot. Instead of owning up to their own weaknesses and shortcomings, they blamed their downfall on Freya.

"Take her!" said one of the Aesir gods. "She's evil. Bind her."

"We will burn her," said Odin. "I will no longer tolerate her corrupting influence."

Freya attempted to pull away from their grip, but found it too strong. "So, you buy my services of your own free will, and then blame me for your own weaknesses? Despite all your cleverness, you are a corrupt lot. You have no true honor if you cannot take responsibility for your own actions."

Three of the gods took Freya to the courtyard and bound her to a post. At the same time, several others brought out kindling and threw it at her feet. Then one of them grabbed a nearby torch and lit the kindling. All the while Freya looked at them, scanning the throng of people with rage in her eyes. Several in the crowd were her own fellow Vanir, but they kept quiet, fearful that they could be next.

Soon, the flames engulfed Freya. She howled in agony and anger. When her body had been reduced to ashes, and the flame had gone, the crowd slowly

Chapter 7— Vanir against the Aesir

In Norse mythology, there were two main groups of gods. The Vanir were like the rustic, Nordic folk who first arrived at the foot of the ice mountains before they melted from the face of northern Europe. The Aesir were like the urban barbarians who built towns and longships.

The Vanir were the folk of Utangard—"beyond the protection of the fence." The Aesir were the folk of Innangard—"within the protection of the fence." Even the names of their realms speak of this difference.

The Vanir were from Vanaheim, while the Aesir were from Asgard. The -gard suffix took on the connotation of fortified places full of laws and order. Even the realm of the humans fell within this protection, for they lived in Midgard. The Vanir, on the other hand, were from that chaotic realm that was both ancient and wild.

Freya's Magic

One of the Vanir goddesses, named Freya, had a special talent for changing destiny. To earn her keep, she went from town to town selling her "art of seidr." When finally she had made her way to Asgard, she was going by the name Heidr, which meant "bright." The powerful Aesir gods appreciated her talents perhaps more than they should. Calling upon Freya to change their fate became a fanatical fad, in some ways like a powerful street drug. The ease of instant gratification is somewhat similar these days to the corruption of our modern youth with fast food diseases and internet theft to guide their morals into darkness. The gods of Asgard were giving up their honor in order to satisfy their basest desires. No longer did they uphold obedience, honor and kin loyalty. They replaced these with a lust for more of Freya's powerful magic.

When the flames had died down and all that was left was a pile of ashes, Odin spoke. "Spread the ashes. Be quick, before she returns."

But she had heard him and leapt from the ashes more powerful than before. After all, she had the skill to change the fates. In that moment, she wished she had the power to change minds, too.

Before the Aesir could regain their wits, some of the Vanir whisked Freya away from the danger and out of the capital city.

Vanir-Aesir War

Naturally, the Vanir gods took this Aesir treachery for what it was and their fear and hatred of these oppressive overlords blew up into a full-fledged war.

On the Aesir side, the gods had superior weapons and their mindless, brute force. The Vanir, however, had powerful magic of every imaginable kind.

Though the powers used on each side were so completely different, they were strangely well matched. Each side suffered and each side won battles, but neither side was winning. In frustration, both sides eventually called a truce.

As tribute to bind them both to the truce, the Vanir offered up Freyr, his sister Freya, and their divorced father, Njörd, to be held by the Aesir as hostage guests. The Aesir offered up Mímir and Hoenir to be held by the Vanir.

Freya, of course, had been at the center of the original dispute. The Aesir gained her powers and that of her brother. The Vanir gained the wisdom of Mímir and Hoenir.

After awhile, though, the Vanir became suspicious of the trade. When Mímir was gone, Hoenir wasn't so wise. In fact, he seemed to be an idiot. Only when Mímir was nearby did Hoenir have his wits. By himself, he was nothing but a burden.

This angered the Vanir. They felt cheated. Instead of complaining to the Aesir or taking their frustrations out on Hoenir, they decapitated Mímir—the valuable part of their exchange. Naturally, they didn't consult Mímir before cutting off his head, but it doesn't take a great deal of wisdom to realize how dumb their act was. Cutting off Hoenir's head would've made far more sense.

But there is something about ancient myths that don't make sense as they are told to us today. Researcher

Rod Martin, Jr. suggests that the truth behind the myth may be something the primitives who repeated the stories did not understand. In an attempt to make their own sense of the ancient stories, they added embellishments that proved illogical, but ended up explaining other elements of the story that made even less sense to them. Thus, the gods, at times, seemed to do things that seemed entirely crazy, but which helped to explain events which the primitive audience could not otherwise understand.

The Vanir sent Mímir's head back to Asgard. There, Odin used magic of his own to restore life to the disembodied head. Frequently, he would ask the head for advice. Behind the nonsense, there may lay a story that makes sense to someone who can imagine the technology the ancients may have had. Perhaps it wasn't a head, but some kind of communications device. But enough speculation.

Both the Vanir and the Aesir were too tired of war to resume their hostilities. Instead, they agreed to come together. Each god then spat into a sacred cauldron and formed from the combined spittle a new being of great wisdom called Kvasir. With this shared creation, they were able to maintain the harmony between them.

There were so many similarities between the stories of Freya and Odin's eventual wife, Frigg, that some scholars have suggested that Freya and Frigg were the same goddess. Could the Vanir goddess finally have forgiven Odin for trying to burn her alive three times? Perhaps so. From the birth of Kvasir, there was peace between the Vanir and the Aesir. Together, they had plenty of enemies and they needed to work together to help maintain order in the universe.

In the next chapter, we take a look at the shape of that universe—organized into 9 realms.

Chapter 8—The Nine Realms

In Norse mythology, the number nine takes on special significance in a number of places, but none more prominent that the fact that the universe was divided into nine specific places.

- Asgard—The realm of the Aesir gods. They were organized, law abiding and brutal.
- Vanaheim—The realm of the Vanir gods. This was a place of rough nature, wild with chaos and lawlessness.
- Midgard—The realm of the humans. This was a middle world in the midst of all the 8 other realms.

- Jotunheim—The realm of the giants.
- Niflheim—A primitive world of ice.
- Muspelheim—A primitive world of fire.
- Alfheim—The realm of the elves.
- Svartalfheim—The realm of the dwarfs or "black elves."
- Helheim—The realm of the dead, ruled over by the goddess Hel.

To the Norse, each of the realms, though invisible to the mortal eye, intersected with some part of Midgard—the Middle Earth, or Middle Fence. For instance, at every graveyard, you could feel the presence of Helheim. In every wilderness area of Midgard, Jotunheim could be felt.

Next, we take a short look at Jotunheim—where the giants lived. And we will explore the deep history of Midgard.

Chapter 9—The Giants and Midgard's Humans

Jotunheim

The giants of Jotunheim were gods who had been banished there by Odin. And they didn't like Odin much, either. Quite often, they were also at odds with the Vanir and the humans of Midgard, too.

Loki was Jotun, but was rescued as an infant and taken home by Odin. So, Loki was the adopted brother of Thor.

Both Freya and her brother Freyr may have been children of a giantess named Skadi. Though some sources point to an unnamed sister of their father as their mother, the poem, Skírnismál, says that Freyr's mother was Skadi and she had once been married to their father, but had divorced because Njörd loved the sea and could not stand the mountains, yet Skadi loved the mountains and could not stand the sea.

Fenrir was the fearsome child of Loki and the giantess named Angrboda. They also produced Hel, the goddess of Helheim, and Jormungang, the giant serpent which circled the earth. Jormungang was also called the Midgard Serpent, because it wrapped itself around the world from within the oceans of Midgard.

Midgard

Throughout the thousands of years following the end of the last glacial period of the current Ice Age, people lived in the lands surrounding the receding glaciers and on the exposed ground which was steadily being claimed by the rising seas. First, there were the Maglemosian people (9000–6000 BC). The massive global warming of 9620–9590 BC had made the northern lands far more hospitable—+7°C in 30 years. Gradually, the Maglemosians were replaced by the Kongemose, Nøstvet and Lihult. In southern Scandinavia, the Kongemose were eventually replaced by the Ertebølle.

Some 5,000 years after the start of the current Ice Age interglacial (Holocene), the Funnelbeaker culture moved into the area of central and northern Europe. These were the last non-Indo-European culture to invade the region. This was what Marija Gimbutas referred to as "Old Europe." They ruled the bulk of Europe for nearly 1,500 years (roughly 4300–2800 BC). In some respects, these were the counterparts in the physical world to the Vanir in the divine realms.

With the invasion of the Corded Ware culture about 2900 BC, Europe became a bit more sophisticated. Eventually, with each progressive wave of influence, the cultures became more orderly with social stratification and formal burial which included worldly artifacts. The artifacts became more refined, including the use of religious icons and instruments of music. These paralleled in our mortal realm, the Aesir in realm of the gods.

But even as human societies were becoming more tame and orderly, so was nature becoming more predictable. Ice Age cold gave way to the Ice Age respite of our current interglacial. Warming brought life to the once lifeless realms. For a brief while, the warmth was so great that even the Sahara saw nearly 3,000 years of green. Only when our world cooled significantly did the Great Desert of North Africa once again lose its hold on life.

With the warmth, violent storms were less frequent. And once the majority of the ice had melted from northern Europe and America, sea levels began to stabilize allowing for coastal settlements to persist.

But like our own world, the realm of the gods was all about change and even their happy, orderly world would come to an end as the forces of chaos gathered their strength.

Greenland's ice cores show a pattern of warm periods. The strongest of these patterns has given us a warm period peak every thousand years, separated by times of relative cooling. Researcher Rod Martin, Jr. has pointed to the dramatic cooling trend of the last 3,000 years as a strong indication that the Holocene may already have started to shut down, in preparation for the next Ice Age glacial period. The broad and deep cold of the Little Ice Age only reinforced this trend. Despite the dire warnings in the corporate media that our world is burning up, the melting of ice is hardly cause for alarm. And our current Modern Warm Period is the coldest of the Holocene's ten, 1,000-year warm periods. Today, the Vikings would not like our

Greenland nearly as much as they liked the far warmer Greenland of Erik the Red and Leif Erikson. In an Ice Age, to fear warmth is madness.

As the Norse gods knew of their own demise in the coming of Ragnarök, we humans should realize that our current, precious warmth will one day also disappear and return us to the chaos of the cold.

The Norse knew cold. They lived alongside the white death and learned to thrive next to it. And when that cold became too much, they responded not by curling up and dying, but by taking the world-at-large and molding it into something more to their liking. It's ironic that today's news media and political bodies of the world are demonizing warmth in an ongoing Ice Age. But perhaps there is great cunning there, too. Like the astute, Norse berserker, perhaps they know something about human nature and about the coming hardships. And perhaps they're playing on the hopes and fears of others in order to gain the upper hand for when the ice returns.

Next, we will take a brief look at dwarfs, elves and the Valkyries.

Chapter 10—Lesser Divine Beings

Dwarfs

The Dwarfs of Norse mythology were not the same "short" people we typically think of when we hear the word. They were black and invisible in the darkness of night or in their natural realm underneath the sunlit world, in a place called Svartalfheim. They were the source of all the finer things used by the gods, humans and others. In this respect they seem similar to Greek myth and the Cyclopes who were imprisoned underneath the Earth in Tartarus. When they were released from captivity, the Cyclopes were so grateful, they fashioned fine things for Zeus (lightning bolts), Hades (cloak of invisibility) and Poseidon (trident).

In Norse mythology, the dwarfs created many of the magical artifacts used by the gods. Freyr, for instance, had a sword that would do the fighting for him. He also had a ship, named Skíðblaðnir, that would always find favorable winds to go wherever its owner wanted to go. His ship could also be folded away and put inside a pocket for later use. And Freyr also had his own pet—the giant, wild boar, Gullinbursti, which would glow in the dark and light the way for its master.

Even Thor's mighty hammar, Mjölnir, was made by the dwarf brothers, Brokkr and Eitri. With it, Thor could topple entire mountains. Though Thor was already far stronger than any mortal, he wore a belt named Megingjörð which doubled his strength. Thor's iron gloves, Járngreipr, allowed him to wield his powerful hammer with ease, despite its shortened handle. Also, the giantess, Gríðr, gave Thor the staff, Gríðarvölr as an added weapon for his defense. All of these were dwarf made artifacts.

Elves

The mortal view of elves has depended largely upon the time and the place. The Norse, for instance, viewed elves as magical and beautiful, especially the "light elves." These creatures were indecisive about humans, for they could either help or hinder the mortals in their aspirations. But to the Germanic tribes farther south, elves were almost always portrayed as malevolent, even monstrous—tricksters who would use their magic to thwart mortals at every turn.

The stories of Norse mythology sometimes conflate elves with dwarfs, frequently swapping terms as if they were synonymous—for instance, the elves or dwarfs of Svartalfheim.

Researcher Rod Martin, Jr. put forth the hypothesis that the ancient myths of magical folk may have come from a real people who may have been the earliest inhabitants of Europe and perhaps the children of a more technological society which disappeared at the end of the last glacial period of the current Ice Age. These were, according to his premise, the refugees of Plato's lost island empire—Atlantis. That island may have given us many elements of myth, including dragons, elves, tales of magic, sorcerers, the Slavic witch, Baba Yaga and others with unnatural powers. While the elves of Norse mythology created magical artifacts used by the gods, the Cyclopes of Greek mythology, who had long been imprisoned in the underworld, made magical artifacts for the Olympian gods. Each of these may be dim memories of real people and real events about which we can only speculate.

Valkyries

The Valkyries were like angels, but sometimes they were entirely evil, planning on who would die in battle, trifling with the lives of mortals without regard to honor or merit. They were servants of Odin, doing his bidding.

Though glamorized by Wagner in his 19th century portrayal of them, the Valkyries were, at times, entirely bloodthirsty. They chose who of the fallen would be able to reside in Valhalla after their death. Valhalla was heaven for the brave, and a training ground for Odin's army in preparation for Ragnarök—

the final confrontation between good and evil—between order and chaos.

In the next chapter, we will take a look at the two most important characters of Norse mythology—Odin and Thor.

Chapter 11—Tales of Odin and Thor

While Odin was king of the gods, Thor was arguably the most beloved. More children seemed to be named after Thor than were named for Odin. Thor was powerful and aggressive like a real man should be, according to their culture. Erik the Red's father was Thorvald ("Thor's ruler"). Two of his children were also named after Thor—Thorvald and Thorstein ("Thor stone"). Leif Erikson's sons were named Thorgils and Thorkell.

Odin

Odin was more of a thinker, seeking wisdom from every place in the nine realms. In fact, Odin once gave one of his eyes in exchange for superior wisdom. As king, he was obligated to know as much as possible about the state of the universe and the major events which occurred therein. Quite often, Odin would leave his home, his wife, Frigg, and his children, in order to gain more insight. He would ride up and down Yggdrasil—the great world tree, many times in disguise.

One day, Odin learned of a great source of wisdom called Mímir's well. Anyone who drank from its waters would receive immense wisdom. This Mímir was also full of wisdom, like his Aesir counterpart, but this one was a giant of Jotunheim, traditional enemies of the other gods and humans. His well was located under the second root of Yggdrasil.

Odin traveled down to the root and found the well guarded by Mímir the giant.

"You!" said Mímir. "Why are you here?"

"I've come seeking wisdom," said Odin.

"Wisdom is a good thing to seek." Mímir nodded in appreciation. "But anything of value does not come without a price. What do you offer?"

Odin thought for a moment. He had not brought anything with him that could be used to barter. His appreciation for wisdom was so great, he was willing to part with most anything, but he had nothing to give in his pockets or satchel. Then, he considered what he had that he could do without. He needed his horse to travel between the realms. But he had two eyes. Could he live with only one? Would Mímir value such a trade?

He chose his words cautiously. "I have an instrument which has gathered a great deal of wisdom. Would you consider trading wisdom for wisdom?"

Mímir smiled at the thought. "Where is this instrument?"

Odin pointed to one of his eyes.

Now, Mímir was delighted. The thought of weakening Odin with the loss of one of his eyes seemed too wonderful to consider. But the king of the Aesir gods knew that such wisdom would be indispensable in the challenges which lay before him.

Thus, Odin gave up one of his eyes in exchange for a sip from the pool of wisdom.

Thor

The Norse god of thunder (thunraz), was seen as the embodiment of courage. Odin was his father, but his mother's name is variously given as Fjörgyn, Hlöðyn or Jord—a giantess of Jotunheim. So, even some of the favorite gods of Norse mythology were children of the Aesir's enemy.

While Thor was the favorite of all the gods, especially amongst the humans of Midgard, Thor's favorite artifact was Mjöllnir, his magic hammer. Not only could he level entire mountains with it, wherever he threw his hammer, it would always return to him. He used his hammer not only in battle, but also at sacred ceremonies. Quite often, he would be called upon to offer his blessings at weddings, even in Midgard. This should not come as a surprise, for Mjöllnir was an instrument of purification. Merely having it at a wedding or other important event somehow lent its power to that event making it pure from the onset.

One day, Thor found that his hammer was missing.

"By Asgard and the nine realms!" Thor's loud voice could be heard throughout the palace. "Where is my hammer?"

Heimdall, who protected the approach to Asgard, offered no explanation for how anyone could have gotten past his vigilant eye. All of Asgard felt the burden of fear, because the most powerful weapon for their protection was now missing.

Frigg (Freya), Thor's step-mother, offered her falcon feathers of transformation so that the hammer could be found. Loki, who had already mastered the art of shape-shifting, used the feathers to accelerate the process. Soon, he left Asgard and headed straight for the likeliest suspect—Thrym, the chief giant of Jotunheim, whose name meant "noisy."

When Loki arrived in Jotunheim, he changed back to his human-like form and asked Thrym about the hammer.

"Mjöllnir?" Thrym chuckled. "Yes, I took it. But I won't tell you how I got past the Aesir's watchdog, Heimdall. I hid the hammer where no one will find it."

"And?" Loki asked. "You must have had a reason for the theft. If you hid the hammer, you must not want to use it, except perhaps as ransom."

Thrym nodded. "That's your giant blood helping you. Very good, Loki. Yes, ransom. For the return of the hammer, I want to marry Freya."

"Odin's wife?"

"That's my price."

"Very well. I will let them know."

At that, Loki gathered up his magic and returned to the form of a falcon—the form revered in Egyptian mythology for its great insight. He traveled back to Asgard.

In the great meeting hall, Loki told of Thrym's demands.

Freya gasped at the thought. She had come to love Odin, her husband, and had cried enough tears when he left on his long journeys to the other realms. The thought of leaving him for another was too much to bear.

The thought of such extortion being leveraged against Asgard alarmed the other gods, as well. Giving in to such ransom would open the door to other treacherous demands.

Feeling guilty for letting Thrym slip past him, Heimdall's mind raced to come up with a solution to this dilemma. "Perhaps," said the great protector, "we could pretend to go through with the marriage. Have Thor go as Freya."

"What?" Thor's voice quaked, shaking the walls of the great hall. "How? Dressed as a woman? You've got to be kidding. That would make me the laughing stock of the universe. That's a ridiculous idea."

"Or," said Loki, "you could let Thrym keep the hammer, and leave us open for attack anywhere in the nine realms. Asgard could fall to the Jotun. How ridiculous would you look, then?"

The hall grew silent as everyone there considered this dark possibility.

Thor swallowed with difficulty. Even he could see the wisdom of putting aside his pride long enough to trick the giant.

"And just think," said Loki, "I could go as one of your handmaidens." He laughed at the thought of also wearing a dress.

"That's easy for you to say," said Thor. "You don't have my reputation to uphold."

"A reputation," replied Loki, "which won't mean much if you don't get back your hammer."

Thor took a deep breath and nodded. "So be it. Let us do this thing. And if anyone laughs at me wearing a dress, they will be the first to feel Mjöllnir's sting."

Everyone in the hall nodded in agreement.

Soon, all of Asgard helped prepare for the big event. Even Odin participated in the ruse by sending out word of his dismay that Freya was leaving him.

Contributions came from all over Asgard for making Thor's wedding dress the most beautiful gown in existence. But everyone kept the secret close. The giants could never discover the deception until it was too late. Soon, they were ready.

As the wedding party made their way down Yggdrasil to Jotunheim, Thor felt great irritation at the beautiful gown he had been forced to wear. His rough hands had been covered by lace gloves, his muscular arms were camouflaged by lovely, embroidered silks, his fierce face was protected by a veil of gold. Járngreipr, his gloves which allowed him to wield the hammer, were tucked away underneath his skirt. He chafed at the disguise and grew more and more anxious to rip it off and to slay the thief and his cohorts.

"Look!" said Thrym. "The gods of Asgard have finally come to their senses. Finally, we get the respect we've long deserved. Come! Let us feast."

All of the preparation and the deception had apparently befuddled Thor's usually sharp mind. At the pre-wedding festivities, he could not contain his hunger. He ate far more than expected for a dainty bride. Thor consumed eight salmon, an entire ox, and even drank several barrels of mead.

Thrym grew suspicious of such a voracious appetite and Loki noticed him watching his bride-to-be.

"I know," said Loki, shaking his head. "She's been so lovesick, she hasn't been able to eat for an entire week, just thinking of you. I'm quite relieved that she's finally eating something."

Thrym nodded cautiously. Then, the image crossed his mind that Freya had been thinking of him—lusting after him—all this time. Suddenly, he felt an overpowering urge to kiss his bride-to-be. Without warning, he reached over and lifted the golden veil enough to peer into her eyes. Thor's glare was all he saw. Perhaps the beard confused him. So surprised was he, that he dropped the veil and sat back in amazement.

Shaking his head, Thrym remarked, "Never have I seen such dreadfully intense eyes."

Loki shook his head and remarked, "Yes, my lord. But doesn't it make sense? A week without eating or sleeping has made her crazy with intense longing."

"Yes, yes!" said Thrym. "By all means. Let's get this wedding going. We need the traditional blessing. We need the hammer." At that, he called forth the hammer.

As Mjöllnir flew through the air toward Thrym, Thor reached under his skirt and donned his magic gloves. Then, he leapt forward and grabbed Mjöllnir's short handle and whirled toward Thrym, bashing him upside the head, ending his life. In rapid succession, while the party guests were still in shock, Thor ended each of their lives.

Weary from battle, Thor was nonetheless happy to shed the dress and to don his own clothes. And not one soul in all of Asgard dared to laugh at Thor's dress.

Next, we learn more about Loki, the trickster god and Ragnarök, the end of times.

Chapter 12—Loki and Ragnarök

Loki

The Norse god of mischief was, in some ways, similar to the Greek god Prometheus. While Prometheus was forever provoking Zeus with his tricks and subterfuge, Loki was forever playing malicious tricks on the other gods of Asgard.

While Prometheus was ultimately chained to a mountain to suffer the perpetual eating of his liver by a giant eagle, Loki was condemned to suffer the continual dripping of poisonous venom on his face for all the evil he had done against the Aesir. But what kind of evil?

Sif, Thor's wife, had long, beautiful hair of gold. Feeling particularly bored, one day, Loki decided to see what would happen if he cut off Sif's fine hair.

Thor wanted to kill Loki for the insult, but the trickster promised that he would ask the dwarfs of Svartalfheim to fashion a far more lovely head of hair.

But later, Loki's mischief also led to the death of Frigg's (Freya's) son, Baldr. He despised the love others held for Frigg's son, Baldr, and he wanted to find some weakness to make Baldr less appealing to his fans. Loki changed his shape so that Frigg would not recognize him. Then, he asked his deadly questions.

"I hear," Loki said in his disguise, "that Baldr is protected from all things. How did you accomplish this?" His voice was one of deep admiration for what Frigg had been able to do.

"Oh, yes," said Frigg. "I asked that every substance promise not to do harm against my son."

"Every substance?" asked Loki. "There were no exceptions?"

"Well, one," Frigg confessed. "Mistletoe, but that is such a simple and innocent plant. No harm could ever come from such a thing."

"So, you didn't get mistletoe to promise not to harm Baldr?"

Frigg nodded.

"But that makes sense," said Loki with encouragement. "I approve of your wisdom."

Later, he fashioned a spear out of mistletoe and gave it to a blind god named Hodr. Loki tricked the unwitting accomplice into throwing the spear, guiding his blind aim toward the hapless young god. When it struck Baldr, the young god immediately died.

Frigg was grief-stricken. After her tears had flowed, she sent a messenger to Hel to beg for Baldr's return.

Hel replied to the messenger, "If Baldr is so beloved, have everyone in the nine realms weep for him. When that happens, I will send Baldr back to Asgard."

The messenger told Frigg and then she sent the messenger throughout the universe to have everyone weep for her son. But when he approached a giantess named Tokk, she said "Let Hel hold what she has! I will not weep for Baldr." Little did the messenger know, but that Tokk was Loki in disguise. Thus, the trickster god made certain that his crime against Baldr was made permanent.

Ragnarök

Unlike the other ancient myths of gods and goddesses, Norse legend included an accounting of the end of times, when the gods themselves would die, and a new age would begin.

Loki's daughter, Hel, had refused to release Baldr, but only because Loki had thwarted every attempt to have Frigg's son released. Both of Loki's sons, Jormungand and Fenrir, had continuously threatened the stability of the universe.

Loki and his fellow giants attacked the Aesir and Vanir gods. Heimdall saw the gathering of giants and blew his horn of alarm.

Freyr and Surt fought and killed one another. Jormungand—the Midgard serpent—battled with Thor, and they killed one another.

Fenrir swallowed Odin. And then, if Garm was another name for Fenrir, as some suspect, he also killed the god Tyr, who had bound Fenrir in an earlier age. Finally, the great wolf was slain by one of Odin's sons, named Vidar.

Heimdall battled with Loki and they died at each other's hand.

After the battle had ended, and the worlds descended into darkness, light gradually returned and two new humans were born. And finally, Baldr returned from Helheim, followed by the rest of the gods to begin the new age.

Conclusion

The story of the Norse gods and Viking heroes gives us great insight into a peoples of the North who survived by both strength and cunning. Not everything they did was admirable, but we can understand much of what happened and of the frailties which molded their behavior.

I hope this work on Norse mythology was able to help you appreciate the complexity of Norse culture and Viking heritage.

Manuscript 3:

Egyptian Mythology

A Fascinating Guide to Understanding the Gods, Goddesses, Monsters, and Mortals

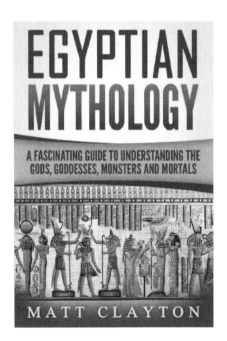

Introduction

From what we know of history, Egypt, along with Sumer, were the foundations of civilization. The Fertile Crescent, which stretched from the Nile Valley to the twin rivers in Mesopotamia, gave us our earliest glimpse of organized man. But organized how? For one, both locations gave us writing—hieroglyphics in Egypt and cuneiform in Sumer. There is still some debate about who was first.

In this book, we will start by looking at the gods and goddesses of Kemet—Ancient Egypt. Then, we will turn our attention to the monsters which likely gave them nightmares and humbled them in their quest to bring order to the world around them. Finally, we will look at the mortals which shaped their civilization and made Egypt the bedrock of our own history. Though Egypt today is only a third-world nation, struggling with terrorism and poverty, their heritage remains vital to the understanding of who we are as a species.

Part 1 — The Gods Come to Egypt

The Book of Knowing The Evolutions Of Ra, and of Overthrowing Apep.

[These are] the; words which the god Neb-er-tcher spake after he had, come into being:

"I am he who came into being in the form of the god Khepera, and I am the creator of that which came into being, that is to say, I am the creator of everything which came into being: now the things which I created, and which came forth out of my mouth after that I had come into being myself were exceedingly many. The sky (or heaven) had not come into being, the earth did not exist, and the children of the earth, and the creeping, things, had not been made at that time. I myself raised them up from out of Nu, from a state of helpless inertness. I found no place whereon I could stand. I worked a charm upon my own heart (or, will), I laid the foundation [of things] by Maat, and I made everything which had form. I was [then] one by myself, for I had not emitted from myself the god Shu, and I had not spit out from myself the

goddess Tefnut; and there existed no other who could work with me."

Legends of the Gods (1912)

E. A. Wallis Budge

Egyptologist and Philologist for the British Museum

Chapter 1 — Osiris, Isis, Seth, and Horus

Perhaps the most important myth of Ancient Egypt is that of Osiris. In it, his wife Isis and his son Horus battled against his brother Seth.

The spellings with which we are most familiar are modern versions of the Greek. The original Egyptian names were more like the following:

- Osiris—Auser

- Isis—Asett

- Seth—Sett

- Horus—Heru

The double "t" at the end of Asett and Sett is not traditional, but it helps to distinguish the name "Sett" from the common English word "set."

Throughout all of Egyptian myth, there is very little actually said about Osiris (Auser) himself. Most of what is said comes after his betrayal by Seth (Sett).

Imagining the Osiris Myth

As they had done for all the ages of man, the priests of the great city of Iunu had crossed over the Ne'weya during the twilight hour after dawn and before sunrise. But this morning vigil at the temple plateau was more somber than usual. All of Kemet was in mourning for their dead ruler, Auser.

The death of a god was not to be taken lightly. Such things tended to throw the entire universe out of balance. Sett had gone over to the dark side of reality. No longer did he stand on the prow of the sun barge, fighting off Apep—the great snake of chaos. Instead, Sett had become chaos. He had betrayed his brother, Auser, and had murdered him. If the priests could believe the rumors, Sett had hacked up Auser's body and flung the parts all up and down the great Ne'weya and its life-giving waters.

As the eastern horizon brightened, the priests performed their daily ritual, burning a handful of grain in sacrifice to the great god, Ra—giver of light. His return to the skies above the mortal realm would be to look upon a world greatly saddened by what had happened to the children of Geb (Earth) and Nut (Heavens). Their offspring, Auser, had been murdered by his brother, Sett. And their offspring, Asett, had been made a widow by the same action.

When the priests had returned to Iunu, they heard the news that Sett had taken control of all Kemet. Asett, Auser's lovely wife, had fled into the hills to the West. Or so people were being told.

Ahmose of Zau made his way into the temple and toward the large meeting hall. Outside the hall, he saw a familiar face. At first, he could not put a name to that visage. Something about it all didn't make sense. What was a beggar doing in the temple at this hour? And why would he recognize a beggar? Then, the truth struck him. That was no beggar, despite the shabby clothes she wore. That was Asett, herself! The goddess was in disguise.

"Your eminence!" said Ahmose, loud enough only to be heard by her. "What are you doing here? It's not safe!"

She turned and bade him to come closer.

"I need your help," she said. "Sett has robbed us all, but especially me. Auser and I wanted to have a son. If we act quickly, it is still not too late. I need for the priesthood to gather all the pieces of Auser. They are to bring them together so that I may perform sacred rites and to consummate the union which was denied us. Our son will become the rightful ruler of Kemet."

Ahmose looked confused, but nodded slowly.

"Why do you hesitate?" she asked.

"I don't doubt your powers, eminence. It's just that Sett is undoubtedly looking for you and I fear for your safety."

"What do you suggest?"

"I am from Zau, here in the Delta. I know of several places where we could bring together the pieces of your husband and find the peace and security required for your ceremony."

"Good. And thank you ..."

"Ahmose, your eminence. My name is Ahmose. I'll see to it right away." He turned to leave.

"One more thing," said Asett. "We also need to have Auser's royal accessories. Do you know of someone who can steal them away from Sett and his forces?"

Ahmose thought for a moment and nodded. "Yes, your eminence. I know of some officers who are still loyal to you and to Auser."

"Thank you, Ahmose."

"My lady." The priest hesitated. "Has Sett become corrupted by Apep?"

The goddess shook her head. "I don't know, yet. Perhaps. He had held that duty for so long, fending off the attacks of chaos. Others have taken over those duties. We can only hope they do as good a job without becoming corrupted."

Within days, all of the pieces had been returned to Lower Kemet and Ahmose had found a warehouse in Zau perfect for the sacred ceremony to be performed.

Within the week, the new god, Heru, had been born, with all the attributes needed to rule. The young god had all the skills of the father and the wisdom of the mother. In addition, Heru had the gift of sight, like his namesake—capable of seeing clearly everything from afar. And like the falcon after which he had been named, Heru also had the swiftness to strike hard at his enemies.

In the first month after his birth, Heru held many battles against his uncle. The young god was so successful in waging combat that Sett feared he might lose the war.

Ever wanting to find an advantage, Sett challenged young Heru to a battle under water.

"We should become as hippopotami and face each other beneath the waves. If either one of us surfaces before three months are up, we will forfeit. Are we agreed?"

To Heru, this seemed reasonable. Soon, they were under water battling against one another.

Asett feared for her son's life and vowed to help him win. From the sky, she hurled massive harpoons at the hippopotamus below, but she had struck the wrong beast.

Heru cried out, "Mother, you have struck me. Please be more careful with your aim."

Asett studied the scene more carefully and soon realized that her son was in pursuit of Sett. There her brother was, several dozen meters ahead.

Several times, she took careful aim, but the harpoon glanced off Sett's wet body. But finally, a harpoon stuck and Sett surfaced.

"Please, dear sister," said Sett, "take pity on your poor brother."

Asett showed her brother mercy and let him heal from his wounds.

Later, Heru confronted his mother. "How could you show him mercy after he tried so many times to kill me?" Suddenly, Heru cut off his mother's head and hid it from her in the mountains to the West.

When Ra, the sun god, heard what Heru had done to his mother, he bound the young god's hands and restored to Asett her head. Then, he gave her a crown of protection so that no one could ever do to her what Heru had done.

But while Heru was bound, Sett swooped in to take advantage of his enemy. Abruptly, he plucked out Heru's eyes and made him blind.

Asett forgave her son for what he had done and wept at what had happened to his eyes. She consulted with Tehuty, the god of wisdom and knowledge. There, she learned that new eyes could be fashioned for Heru from the old arts. Soon, Heru could see again. Once more, he went on the offensive, taking every opportunity to beat his uncle in battle.

Again, it looked as though Sett would lose everything, partly because his sister, Asett, was interfering in his war against Heru.

Sett made his way to the great council of gods—the Ennead. There, he begged the council for a meeting to discuss with Heru their differences, but without the interference of Asett.

They agreed to a meeting. So, Sett sent out word to Heru that he wanted to meet at the Island of the Middle Ground and let the Ennead judge between them. And Sett commanded the ferryman not to let anyone of the likeness of Asett to journey to that island.

The following day, the council met. There, Sett and Heru presented their cases while the council listened. In the meantime, Asett disguised herself as an old woman and bribed the ferryman with a gold ring so that she may pass to the Island of the Middle Ground.

When she arrived, she turned herself into a young maiden so that she could distract Sett and help him to fail. As she served the guests more wine, she caught Sett's eye and he called her near.

"My Lord Sett," she said. "I am so grateful for all you have done. Your bravery makes my own hardship seem more durable."

"Hardship?" replied Sett with concern. "What could make such a beautiful woman less than happy?"

"An intruder has invaded my home, killed my husband, and stolen my son's birthright."

"Damn him!" exclaimed Sett. "The man should be publicly executed for his crimes. We shall do that immediately."

"No, please!" she replied. "Do not kill him. I would never wish to have anyone's blood on my own hands. Banishing him from the land would be sufficient to set my heart at ease."

"Then," said Sett loudly, "he shall be banished."

"Thank you, my Lord Sett. For the home is Kemet, my husband was Auser, my son is Heru, and the intruder to be banished is you!"

Suddenly, Sett realized that this young wench was none other than his pesky sister. His own words had condemned himself and all in front of Heru and the gods of the Ennead. He was outraged.

Asett flew away, calling out her words to mock her brother. "You have condemned yourself, dear brother. What say you?"

"The ferryman should be punished," said Sett. So, the next day, Sett had the toes on both the ferryman's feet cut off because he had disobeyed Sett's command not to let Asett across.

Heru soon won the war and banished Sett from Kemet for all time.

Chapter 2 — The Sun and Creation

Similar to the myths of some other cultures, Egyptian creation stories talk of a time before creation which was filled with void and chaos—an expanse called "Nu."

To the Egyptians, the beginning of all things was *Zep Tepi* ("first occasion"). The void itself was described as a primordial body of water out of which rose up a mound shaped like a pyramid—a *benben*. This word is similar to the name given to the sacred bird of rebirth (compare Greek phoenix), the bennu.

From the ancient city of Khemenu (known to the late Greek rulers of Egypt as Hermopolis), their story of creation starts with the formation of eight gods of the Ogdoad.

Nu was male and his female mate was Naunet. Together, they represented the dead, primordial sea.

Huh was male and his female mate was Hauhet. Together, they represented the infinite expanse of that ancient sea.

Kuk was male and his female mate was Kauket. Together, they represented the dim murkiness which was a natural part of that primeval fluid.

Amun was male and his female mate was Amaunet. Together, they represented the opaque obscurity of that earliest of waters. This quality made it impossible to discover more about the water's nature.

With all of them filled with the theme of water, it should be no surprise that they were symbolized as frogs (male) and water snakes (female).

When the Ogdoad came together, an imbalance was created which forced the emergence of the first benben, and from it, the appearance of the sun to give its light to all of material existence.

From the ancient city of Iunu (known to the late Greek rulers of Egypt as Heliopolis), the creation story takes on a somewhat different form.

To the people of Iunu, Atum created himself out of the watery void. In some versions, Atum is seen sitting on the primordial benben; in others, he is the benben itself. Atum represented the setting sun—where the day reaches its completion.

It's interesting to note that the Hebrews also viewed sunset as the end of the day and the moment after the sun disappears as the beginning of a new day.

Because of Atum's association with the sun, he was sometimes called Ra or Atum-Ra. Like many of the myths in other cultures, the gods are frequently described as if they have human-like form. For instance, Atum either masturbates or sneezes his first two children into existence. They are the god of air, Shu, and the goddess of moisture, Tefnut.

The First Tragedy in Creation

While Atum was working on one of his many creation projects, both Shu and Tefnut took an interest in their environment.

"What is this watery substance surrounding the island of creation?" asked Shu.

"Father did not say much about it. Only that it was here before he arrived."

"Aren't you curious about it?"

"Well," replied Tefnut, "perhaps a little. What did you have in mind?"

"Father's busy. We shouldn't disturb him." Shu nodded, gaining confidence in his new decision. "Perhaps we should explore it. Maybe, if we find something of value out there, we can bring it back to Father for him to use."

Tefnut smiled and also nodded. Abruptly, she jumped into the primordial waters and swam away. Shu followed close behind.

Later, when Atum was ready for a break, he called for his children, but did not hear a reply. Soon, he became frantic. Creation was still brand new and Atum was still learning how to deal with the nature of reality and how to shape its form. Was there something he had missed? Could there be something in the tools with which he was working that created destruction? Then, he noticed a residual swirl in the primordial waters. In an instant, he knew his children had dove into those waters and had swum away.

"Oh! My dear children." He feared that they might become lost in the murky gloom of that infinite void.

His light would not reach infinity. They would not be able to see it if they swam too far.

"What to do?"

All of a sudden, thought and action became one. He plucked out his right eye and cast it into the void. "Find my children!" was the commandment and divine intention.

Not long afterward, this new goddess—the Eye of Ra—returned with the children in tow.

Atum was so relieved that he wept and each teardrop became a new creation, each one an individual human being.

The Supreme Council of Gods

After Atum had worked a while at creating the world and many of the new gods he had needed to help manage all of physical reality, he established a supreme council of gods called the Ennead. Its nine members were Atum-Ra and his two children, Shu and Tefnut, and their two children, Geb and Nut, and their four children, Auser, Asett, Sett, and Nephthys.

In contrast to the Ogdoad, which dealt primarily with the void of chaos, the Ennead handled physical existence.

More Creation Stories

From the ancient city of Inbu-Hedj (known to the late Greek rulers of Egypt as Memphis), their story of creation involves the patron god of all craftsmen, Ptah. Here, the physical world was carefully crafted with intellectual precision, unlike the accident of Khemenu's creation myth, or the sneeze of Iunu's creation story.

Ptah possessed an innate ability to see a desired end result in all its details and to find all the necessary resources for its fabrication.

Egyptian myth placed the mental faculties in the heart, rather than in the brain. It was said that when Ptah spoke from the heart, the things he visualized became manifest in physical reality. As he would speak the name of something, it would suddenly appear. His spoken word was the source of all other gods, physical objects, and mortal beings.

At creation, Ptah was connected to Tatjenen, the god of the first benben.

In some respects, Ptah is similar to the Abrahamic God of Judaism and Christianity where creation was more an activity of intelligent intention. In some other respects, Ptah's method of creation—from the heart—mimics the nature of prayer. Philosopher Rod Martin, Jr. notes, "Prayer, when done right, comes from feeling or 'the heart.' It never comes from thought or the words on someone's lips. A fearful heart, asking for salvation, will receive more to fear. A confident, but humble heart, asking for anything, will receive that thing instantly. And most people are not too confident about instantly, so time (delay) becomes part of the delivery."

From the ancient city of Waset (known to the late Greek rulers of Egypt as Thebes, and in modern times, Luxor), we receive still another version of creation. To them, Amun was an invisible force behind every aspect of creation and also an element of the Ogdoad. Amun's form encompassed everything—from beyond the deepest underworld, and the highest of the heavens.

When Amun uttered his first cry, it shattered the sameness of the infinite nothingness and gave birth to both the Ogdoad, and its eight gods, but also the Ennead, and its nine gods.

To the people of Waset, Amun was a mystery shrouded in darkness for even all of the other gods. And the attributes and skills of all the other gods were merely one aspect or another of Amun. The inhabitants of Waset considered their city to be the location of the original benben.

The Sun—A Pivotal Aspect of Creation

Central to all of these stories is the appearance of the sun. All of Kemet (Egypt) worshiped at least one aspect of the sun. In fact, Heliopolis was literally "sun city."

When Atum plucked out his eye in order to find his children, Shu and Tefnut, that new goddess not only had the ability to perceive, but also the ability to cast the necessary light on her surroundings in order to see more clearly. The Eye of Ra has been represented throughout Egyptian myth by various goddesses. The list is long and includes Bastet, Hathor, Mut, Sekhmet, and Wadjet. This "eye" was sometimes symbolically represented as the solar disk. On the back of the

American dollar, it may also be the eye in the benben that is glowing above a truncated pyramid.

A number of gods were more directly associated with the sun. Of course, there is Ra, who represented the sun at or near zenith, when its blazing light does most of its work in nourishing the plants of the physical world.

Naturally, the sun has different aspects to its daily cycle. Khepri took the first visible slot of the day as the sun rose. Because of this "newborn" state, he also represented rebirth.

The lesser god, Aten, represented the perceptible disk of the sun, but not any of its life-giving warmth or light.

As we've already seen, Atum represented the setting sun, which ties in thematically with his status as a source of creation. The setting sun completes each day, and Atum was able to complete each creation by giving it form, substance, and persistence.

And Ptah was long associated with the sun after it set. During each night, the sun replenished itself, preparing for the new day. Besides his skills as a craftsman, Ptah was also a god of the arts and biological creation (fertility).

Chapter 3 — Gods and Humans

As we saw earlier, humans had not remained satisfied with the status quo. To a few upstarts, harmony was boring. Those few wanted something more. They were not content to follow Maat, the goddess of order.

Ra was no fool. He realized that humans would one day get restless and attempt something similarly stupid. Up until that time, life had existed in a state of perpetual sameness called *djet*. By creating a dichotomous existence called *neheh,* his mortal children would have some variety to their existence. They would have day and night, the monthly cycles, and the seasons of the year.

Ra also reasoned that having his rule on Earth made him and his court a tempting target. Because of this, Ra made another drastic change.

"Shu?"

"Yes, my Lord Father."

"As god of the air, I want you ..."—Ra turned to the others of court waiting in attendance—"... and you, you, all eight of you. I want you all to lift up Nut, goddess of the sky. Hold her aloft so that we can reside far above the humans."

"Because of their selfishness?" asked Tefnut.

"Yes, my darling child. The human selfishness will now have no way to reach us."

"But can we rule the world effectively from such a distance?" asked Sett, one of the sons of Nut.

"I'm glad you brought that up," replied Ra. "Because you've been busy helping me ferry the sun across the sky, I will give the job of local rule to your brother, Auser. He and his wife, Asett, will take charge of Kemet and manage affairs there. We'll never be far away and we can all move in to intervene, if needed."

Auser stepped forward and asked, "Lord Ra, do you have any advice for me before I begin my task?"

"Keep the order of things. The society of Kemet shall remain rigid. Every individual is to do that to which they were assigned and into that which they were born. To vary from this is to invite chaos. Without this control, all manner of surprising things could happen. We cannot allow great change. I have given them enough variety with the days, the months, and the yearly cycles."

And so, Nut was lifted into the sky and the gods ruled from on high. Auser descended to Kemet and took charge of the land as Ra had commanded. But humans were not the only ones who felt the lure of temptation.

As Auser and Asett left the presence of the other gods, Sett looked on and wished he had that job, instead of standing on the prow of the sun barge every day, hacking at each threat from Apep.

Part 2 — Monsters of Egypt

"Apep, the serpent-devil of mist, darkness, storm, and night, of whom more will be said later on, and his fiends, the 'children of rebellion,' were not the result of the imagination of the Egyptians in historic times, but their existence dates from the period when Egypt was overrun by mighty beasts, huge serpents, and noxious reptiles of all kinds. The great serpent of Egyptian mythology, which was indeed a formidable opponent of the Sun-god, had its prototype in some monster serpent on earth, of which tradition had preserved a record; and that this is no mere theory is proved by the fact that the remains of a serpent, which must have been of enormous size, have recently been found in the Fayyum."

E. A. Wallis Budge

Keeper of the Egyptian and Assyrian Antiquities in the British Museum

The Gods of the Egyptians, vol.I, 1904

Chapter 4 — Apep: Great Snake of Chaos

There weren't too many true monsters in Egyptian mythology, unlike the myths of many other cultures. The Norse had their Kraken and great wolf, Fenrir. The Greeks had their Scylla, Charybdis, Echidna, and Typhon. In Egypt's lore, the only true monster was chaos which took the form of a giant snake. Its name was Apep (Apophis in Ancient Greek). We will look more closely at this creature in a moment.

Fearsome Gods of Egypt

Many of the gods of Egyptian mythology could, at times, be fearsome, but quite often it was to the enemies of Egypt (Kemet) or to those who had done great evil.

For instance, Am-heh, with a name that meant either "eater of eternity" or "devourer of millions," had the head of a dog and body of a human, and lived on a lake of flame in the underworld. If you got on his bad side, no one but the god Atum-Ra could calm him down. But this was only another reason to live a good and righteous life.

Early in the history of the universe, Ra discovered that his mortal children—humans—had grown dissatisfied with peace and order. They wanted to overthrow Ra, the ruler of the universe, and were plotting to take his place. This deeply troubled Ra that his creation would be working with chaos to upend the order of things.

"What shall I do?" Ra asked of his fellow gods. "It's all I and Sett can do to hold off Apep when I bring light to the world each day."

"What should we do with anyone who threatens creation?" asked Hathor. "A criminal must be punished."

"Or eliminated," said Shu.

Ra brooded for a moment and finally nodded, turning to Hathor. "Do you have a suggestion?"

Hathor started to reply, but Tefnut spoke instead. "Hathor's daughter, Sekhmet, could slaughter them. She seems well suited for that kind of task. As a lioness, she can hunt them down and devour them."

Ra took a deep breath and said, "Sekhmet, come forth. I have need of your talents."

The lion goddess moved forward to stand before Ra. "Yes, your eminence. How may I serve you?"

"The humans have become egocentric. Their selfishness threatens the very fabric of all creation. I want you to devour them all. Remove their kind from the world."

"I understand, Lord Ra. But do you realize that once I start, the bloodlust will blind me to any other needs and plug my ears to any other requests?"

"I understand," replied Ra. "Let it be done. Begin now."

So, Sekhmet turned from the Ennead and all those gathered in attendance. She went out to the world at large and began slaughtering every human that she could find—man, woman, and child. With her claws, she slashed at their bodies, spilling their blood over everything. She would wallow in that blood and then drink it up. The carnage had begun.

The following day, as Ra moved the sun across the sky, with Sett at the prow of his barge to fend off Apep, he looked down at the world. From even there, he could hear the wailing. He could smell the fear and death.

"Tehuty?" said Ra, turning to the god of wisdom and knowledge. "What do you think of this thing that Sekhmet does below us?"

"While it is true that many of the humans were plotting to overthrow the gods, including you, my Lord, there were some who possessed righteous hearts. Certainly, those who held chaos in their hearts should be punished, but—"

"But you think it was wrong to kill them all."

Tehuty nodded.

"And Maat? What do you say about all this?"

The goddess of order took several moments to gather her thoughts before speaking. She knew that quick words could create their own chaos. "My Lord, what you have started has its own wisdom. Certainly, the humans have now grown fearful of the gods and many have become repentant for their conspiracies. And I agree that a few were never so treasonous as to deserve such a painful death. If only there were some way to keep a few of the humans to see if the threat of extinction has made them sufficiently humble."

"But how?" asked Ra. "Sekhmet said herself that she is unstoppable now that she has started drinking up the blood. Would it be valuable to save a few? They had such potential."

Tehuty nodded. "Saving a few, my Lord, would be a good thing. How? Perhaps we could make Sekhmet drunk so that she would forget her bloodlust."

Ra laughed and shook his head. "Brilliant suggestion, but how would you carry it out? I don't see her slowing down to indulge in such things."

"She seeks only blood," said Sett. "Give her more blood."

"Yes," said Ra. "Make seven thousand jugs of beer. Thicken them and add a color to make them look much as blood. Then pour the beer onto the land before her so that she drinks it up instead of the blood."

By the next day, the jugs of beer had been brewed, thickened, and colored. All of the gods helped to pour the red liquid before the rampaging Sekhmet. Sure enough, she stopped to drink it all and when she was done, she walked a few more paces and sleepily lay down to rest. When she awoke, Ra was there to give her a new command.

"My dearest Sekhmet," said Ra.

"My Lord," she replied, looking away as if burdened by a considerable guilt. "I feel my task is not yet complete."

"But it is," said Ra. "You have done well and I now need a few of the humans to remain alive so that they may learn humility from what you have accomplished."

"I understand."

And so, Sekhmet had become a scourge to humanity, but only for a brief while. Mankind had called her wrath upon itself.

The Meaning of Apep

Before creation, all was chaos—without form or purpose. This was known as Apep, and it took the form of a giant snake.

It was the job of the gods to dispel the darkness of chaos and to replace it with order and light.

Occasionally, Sett would become overwhelmed while attending to the prow on Ra's barge. Apep would attempt to swallow the sun, blotting out its light, but always Sett would regain control of the situation, repel Apep and restore the light of the sun.

In the world of reason and science, we know that the "swallowing" of the sun was merely an occurrence of a solar eclipse by the Moon. The order of our physical universe is merely the result of physical law's constancy and continuity.

Throughout Egyptian history, the pharaohs were agents of the sun in dispelling the chaos of the uncivilized folk who were always attempting to invade their lands. In many ways, those uncivilized people were agents of Apep, destroying the order of things. Thus, all of the Egyptian gods were monsters to the enemies of Kemet and to the instruments of Apep.

Chapter 5 — Sett: God of Desert, Storms, War, Evil, and Chaos

Sett was not always a bad guy. Originally, he was a member of the Ennead—the council of gods.

After Sekhmet had destroyed most of humanity, Ra had the gods lift Nut (sky) far from the Earth. There, the gods would rule over the world from afar. In order to maintain order locally, however, Ra set Auser (Osiris) as ruler over Kemet and Asett, as his wife, to rule with him.

Sett grew jealous, for even the gods were not above becoming self-centered and selfish. One might wonder if Sett had had too many close calls with Apep. Had he become tainted with Apep's intent—to subvert order with chaos?

So, throughout all of Egyptian myth, only Apep and Sett may be considered true monsters, for their intent was against that of peace and order, and toward self-concern and selfish need.

Seduced by Power and the Dark Side

A new day had begun. Ra was once again commanding his barge across the sky, towing the image and likeness of the sun to shine its light upon the world below. With him were Maat, the goddess of order, and Tehuty, the god of wisdom and knowledge. At the prow stood Sett, sword at the ready to strike against Apep should the great serpent attempt to interfere.

The sameness of this event made Sett a little crazy. Here he was, perched on the divine barge, doing the same thing over and over again, every day of the year, and every year, one after the other.

Below, he could see the humans and their varied activities. Some were coming together to build their separate civilizations. Sett admired the activity and the consequences of such building. He liked the sense of change and progress.

Then, Sett caught a glimpse of Asett and Auser, ruling over the greatest nation of the world—Kemet. The ribbon of water, which snaked through the desert, glistened as it reflected the sun's light back up at him and at the other members of the divine barge.

"What is it like to rule?" he wondered. "What is it like to command others and to have them do your bidding?"

And as he wondered, he didn't see that Apep was circling the barge, looking for an opportunity to strike.

"Sett!" yelled Ra. "What are you doing? Apep has taken a bite out of the sun."

The younger god blinked several times and looked back toward the sun. Indeed, part of it had already become darkened and in the glare of the light that remained, he could see the shadowy form of Chaos writhing through the sky. Immediately, he struck at the beast, but it would not let go.

The sky became increasingly dark until all of the sun's light had been snuffed out. Repeatedly, Sett struck at the beast and finally drove his blade into its heart.

Slowly, Apep gave up its prize and light returned to the world.

Minutes later, he could see the eternal snake slithering away across the universe.

"Well done, my son," said Ra. "Again, you have prevailed against Chaos."

Sett nodded at the praise, but felt empty. Moments before, he had felt his own heart pounding with the excitement of conflict in action. Now, all returned to the sameness of boring order and tranquility.

Why couldn't I have more conflict in my life? Sett asked of himself. To feel the excitement of a life-threatening challenge.

As Sett mulled over these dark thoughts, his eyes drifted once again down to the Great Hall from where Auser ruled over all of Kemet. "If I had his power, I'd use it to conquer other lands. That would be enough excitement to last several millennia."

Later, as the day came to its completion, and the divine barge was taken over by the maintenance crews of the night, Sett wandered toward Kemet to pay his brother and sister a visit. The closer he got, the darker his heart became, and the more he resented that they had what he now desperately wanted.

The god of defense had now been seduced by the desire to attack. Halfway to Kemet, he stopped. There, in the bright, starlit desert, he pondered how he might achieve his deepest desires. But betrayal would not be easy. The remainder of the night he spent plotting against his brother and sister.

As the clarion call came for him to return to the divine barge, he looked down at his right arm and felt the blood coursing through his own veins. In his mind's eye, he could see Apep swimming through his veins, giving his life new meaning.

Over the next several weeks, Sett talked in veiled language to many of the lesser gods and to some of the more powerful humans of Kemet. From his many conversations, he was able to discern the hearts of those who would be willing to help him in his quest for power. Over those many days, he built an army of like-minded who desired change—the same magnitude of change which had turned the universe from a realm of chaos into one of order.

Then, one day, Sett did not show up when the call came to board the barge of the sun.

"Where is Sett?" asked Ra.

"I do not know, my Lord," replied Tehuty.

"Neither do I," said Maat. "What will we do?"

"We will take turns warding off Apep," said Ra with growing certainty. "We must maintain the order of time. The day must have its period of sunlight. We will find Sett later, when our work in the sky is done."

About mid-morning, Tehuty was standing guard at the prow of the barge when he was distracted by a flurry of motion below.

"Ra!" he shouted. "Look! It's Sett. He's attacking Kemet."

Ra looked down in horror as Sett and his mighty forces swept across Kemet, destroying the armies of Auser.

And as Sett approached the capital city, Auser came out to meet with his brother.

"Why do you do this, brother?" asked Auser. "Why aren't you on the divine barge guarding the sun?"

A dark smirk crossed Sett's face as he replied, "Just as Ra saw the changes that brought order to the universe, I am overseeing the changes that will demonstrate power and control in the universe."

"At what cost?" asked Auser. "You are destroying order. Apep will surely have an advantage if you continue."

"I know how to handle Apep," said Sett. "After all, I've been fighting back chaos for thousands of years. No one is more qualified than I."

"But—"

"Take him!" commanded Sett.

And the minions of Sett took Auser and bound him.

"Brother, I do this for the good of the universe." Abruptly, Sett began hacking at his brother's body, cutting it into more than a dozen pieces. Then, he turned to his chiefs and commanded them, "Each of you take a piece of my brother and take it to a major city of Kemet. This way, Auser will no longer have power over Kemet."

The rest of the gods were shocked by what Sett had done, but his bold actions also engendered for him a measure of respect from nearly all of the divine beings. The only one not so touched by admiration was, of course, Auser's sister and wife, Asett.

Part 3 — Egyptian Mortals Who Shaped History

Ozymandias

I met a traveller from an antique land,
Who said—"Two vast and trunkless legs of stone
Stand in the desert. . . . Near them, on the sand,
Half sunk a shattered visage lies, whose frown,
And wrinkled lip, and sneer of cold command,
Tell that its sculptor well those passions read
Which yet survive, stamped on these lifeless things,
The hand that mocked them, and the heart that fed;
And on the pedestal, these words appear:
My name is Ozymandias, King of Kings;
Look on my Works, ye Mighty, and despair!
Nothing beside remains. Round the decay
Of that colossal Wreck, boundless and bare
The lone and level sands stretch far away."
—Percy Bysshe Shelley, 1818, *The Examiner* of London

Chapter 6 — Imhotep, the 27th Century BC Polymath

Five hundred years after what modern historians call the "First Dynasty"—after the first Scorpion King—and nearly four hundred years after Narmer the Great had unified all of Kemet, Djoser ruled the land of the sacred river. He ruled from Inbu-Hedj ("the white walls"), a city that would be known to the Greeks as Memphis.

A man named Imhotep assisted the pharaoh and proved to be so indispensable that he had earned the right to be called "first in line after the king."

Kenneth Feder, anthropologist and professor of archaeology, lists the official titles of Imhotep in one of his books: "Chancellor of the King of Egypt, Doctor, First in line after the King of Upper Egypt, Administrator of the Great Palace, Hereditary nobleman, High Priest of Heliopolis, Builder, Chief Carpenter, Chief Sculptor, and Maker of Vases in Chief."

Imhotep was also a poet and philosopher who was frequently quoted throughout most of Egyptian history.

So, it seems, Imhotep was what we would call a polymath, or "Renaissance man." His knowledge was broad, stretching across many fields. His skills were varied and of great depth, so that he may be compared favorably with the likes of Leonardo da Vinci, Galileo Galilei, and Johann Wolfgang von Goethe.

This right-hand man to the king was also a mathematician, astronomer, and architect. It is said that he designed the first pyramid—the Step Pyramid at Saqqara.

By the time of the Roman Republic, Imhotep had been elevated to the status of a god. His medical works were used during the Roman Empire and were so highly thought of that two Roman emperors (Tiberius and Claudius) had temple inscriptions include praise for Imhotep.

Imhotep the Master Planner

The king's chancellor went to bed tired, but happy. He had accomplished a great many things with his time in service to all of Kemet and to the resident god, Djoser, emissary of Heru, and representative of the Ennead on Earth.

Outside his darkened bedroom, the stars filled the sky with a warm glow. Unlike most men, Imhotep looked at every part of existence as a resource and as a source of solutions. While the field of stars held the world, he held his wife and drifted off into a deep sleep.

During his dreams, he remembered the concern discussed by his king earlier in the day—that the grain harvest this year was noticeably less than that of the previous year. Then, as dreams so easily do, he turned once and found himself seven years into the future, after as many years of plenty. The people were becoming fat with prosperity. He turned once more and found himself another seven years into the future, but this time many of his people were dead or dying. Those who remained were thin from starvation.

The next moment, he found himself sitting upright in bed. The bedding was cold and clinging. Sweat dripped down his face from the anguish he had felt moments before.

"What is it, my love?" asked his wife. "Is something wrong?"

"No, my beloved. Go back to sleep. Everything is as it should be."

The chancellor got up and crossed the room to the outer hall. So as not to awaken his wife, he called quietly to his slave, "Fetch a flame for my lantern. I need to write some notes for the coming daylight."

In moments, the slave had returned and lit Imhotep's lantern and the chancellor then went to his study to write down the thoughts that were coming to him.

For a moment, he sat there merely looking at the papyrus and the reed pen he held, ready for ink.

"Look at the problem," he whispered to himself. "What exactly is its nature? What is there behind the feeling I have?"

He nodded. "Famine. Prevention."

Quickly, he opened the small clay jar and dipped his reed pen into it, drawing into it some of the ink.

Deftly, he stroked the papyrus surface, combining the symbols which grew in meaning to match the thoughts in his mind. In moments, he had captured the gist of his concerns and had made a list of possible solutions. The most promising such solution seemed to be that of storing surplus in years of plenty and rationing that storage when needed.

When done, he held the papyrus sheet up and admired its contents. Such a simple idea, it's a wonder no one had considered it ever before. He half laughed at the ironic thought that this brilliant idea may have come too late. What if next year's harvest begins years of famine?

He shrugged and smiled. No sense worrying. "Worry," he whispered to himself, "is a wasted effort about something that might not happen. Better to enjoy the moments we have and to make the best of them."

With that, he took the papyrus and the lamp, and returned to his bedroom. After placing the valuable writing in a safe place on a side table, he blew out the lantern and returned to bed and to his wife.

This time, as he drifted off to sleep, he felt the happiness of that rare kind of person who always finds solutions to the problems of this mortal world. He knew his own intelligence was substantial, but that alone had not made him chancellor to King Djoser. There were others more intelligent than he, but they lacked his humble attitude and his child-like imagination.

When the sun returned the following morning, Imhotep broke his fast, then kissed his wife before leaving for the palace main.

When he arrived at the king's side, he waited until the pharaoh had finished his daily routine.

"Any new business?" Djoser asked his counselor.

"Yes, my Lord," said Imhotep. "I have a suggestion on the topic we discussed yesterday—concerning the shortage of grain harvest."

King Djoser tilted his head to the side and squinted his eyes. An expression of growing interest covered his face.

"There is a certain minimum amount we need to keep our nation healthy. I propose that we store all grain beyond that minimum until we have seven years of surplus. This way, the unpredictable nature of Nile flooding will never threaten our survival. We will always have enough to keep us alive and thriving until the years of abundance return to us."

Sudden laughter startled Imhotep. He shook his head and moved backward one step. Then, he looked upon his king's smiling face and returned his own smile.

"Very good, my friend," said Djoser. "Very, very good. My faith in you was well placed. You continue to contribute far more to Kemet than any counselor who has come before. For that reason, I hereby proclaim you to be my second-in-command. Whenever I am away, your words will be as my own. So it shall be done."

Imhotep bowed to his king and felt greatly humbled by the honor bestowed on him. He accepted the honor graciously, but inwardly prayed that he would always live up to that honor—that he would continue to have the creativity and wisdom to do for Kemet, and for his king, what needed to be done.

Chapter 7 — Akhenaten, the King Who Upended Tradition

Amenhotep IV was the second son of Amenhotep III. The father had been a highly successful pharaoh—the ninth of the Eighteenth Dynasty, reigning from 1388–1351 BC. More statues were found of the father than any other Egyptian king.

Amenhotep IV's older brother, Thutmose, was destined to be king after his father, but in the 30th year of the elder's reign, Thutmose died. Suddenly, Amenhotep IV was to become the father's successor (1351–1334). And in the 37th year of the father's rule over Egypt, the father died. All that power and prosperity went to the second son. Was there foul play? We have no way of knowing. The records about the successor are scarce.

We do know that in the fifth year of his reign, Amenhotep IV changed his name to Akhenaten. The name he had shared with his father—Amenhotep—meant "Amun is satisfied," in honor of the god whose name meant "invisible" or "the hidden one." The new name meant "effective for Aten." And Aten was a sun god, referring to the solar disk, rather than the other aspects of the sun—its light, heat, giving of life, and dividing the day from the night.

For 200 years, Amun had retained national popularity as one of Egypt's most important deities. Before that, Amun had been only a local deity. But when the city of Waset (later named Thebes by the Greeks) was made the capital of unified Egypt, what was local had become national. In those ten generations, the high priests of Amun had gained great power and influence. Now, this one king who was not even supposed to have been king, was turning his back on this supreme god, in favor of some minor angel barely mentioned in the ancient texts.

At first, Akhenaten was tolerant of the religious beliefs of others. But gradually, he began to put more and more pressure on departing from the old ways. He used the wealth of Egypt to build a new capital which he called Akhetaten (modern Amarna) at a place where nothing had ever been built before—an entire city constructed in the wilderness from zero.

During his reign, Egypt lost a considerable area from its northern holdings to the Hittites. Some felt that this king was dabbling in chaos and that the losses were from the sins of chaos. Certainly, the Amun priests of Waset would have found this idea popular.

Akhenaten had several wives, as was the tradition of pharaohs. His Great Royal Wife, or chief consort, was Nefertiti. Other wives included Kiya, Meritaten, Ankhesenamun, and a sister whose name is unknown, but who is called "The Younger Lady" by historians.

Nefertiti gave her husband only daughters—six of them.

Imagining Akhenaten

The grand vizier moved slowly toward the throne and bowed. As he did so, he lifted up several clay tablets.

"Approach," said Akhenaten. "What do we have here?"

"Reports, my Lord," said the grand vizier. "From your vassal states in Canaan."

The king lifted his right hand and curled his fingers as if to summon the vizier to come closer. But the man knew better that the meaning was to elicit more facts.

"Yes, your eminence," said the vizier. "These are pleas from Rib-Hadda for military assistance and—"

"Again?" Akhenaten shook his head in disbelief. "That one administrator sends more messages to me than all the others combined. If he loses his position in Byblos from a coup, I will welcome it, just so long as his successor continues to pay tribute to the Empire. Right now, I'm more concerned with our campaign in Nubia. Any word from there?"

"Not yet, your eminence."

Akhenaten took a deep breath and waited a moment more. "Any other affairs of state to discuss?"

"Thankfully no, my Lord. But the Great Royal Wife and your six daughters wish to see you."

"Nefertiti," replied the king. "Yes, please. Send them in."

After Akhenaten

All in all, Akhenaten ruled Egypt for 17 years. After Akhenaten died, Smenkhkare became the new king and he ruled for something like one year. Very little is know about him, because later kings tried to erase from history every record of Akhenaten and everyone associated with him. Smenkhkare may have been a son of Akhenaten or a brother; we simply do not know.

After Smenkhkare, a woman sat on the throne. She was named Neferneferuaten. She ruled for about two years. Was she Nefertiti, or one of Akhenaten's daughters by Nefertiti (Meriaten or Neferneferuaten Tasherit)? We do not know this, either.

Imagining King Tut

All of Akhetaten was in mourning, officially, but secretly many rejoiced that another member of the sacrilegious family had died. Neferneferuaten had ruled for one year and nine months, but the priest of Amun made certain that every one of her orders had been thwarted in one fashion or another.

Some say that the stress of her inability to command finally got to her. Others say that the vizier who died at the same time had sacrificed himself in order to poison her last meal. He had tasted it, showing that it was safe, but according to some, it was a slow-acting poison that the vizier himself had used.

Today, the funeral had ended. Neferneferuaten had now been buried in her makeshift tomb. Before the crowds stood a young boy of nine. Behind him stood the new grand vizier, his assistants, plus several cousins and the boy's mother, known to historians only as The Younger Lady. Today, Tutankhaten the boy would become King Tut, ruler over all of Kemet— from Nubia to Canaan, and from Libya to the Red Sea. After the crowning ceremony, the vizier whisked the young boy into council chambers. Surrounding the boy were a host of counselors, scribes, and junior viziers. All of them were adherents of Amun, the one true god of Egypt—the most supreme god which had no form. Compared to him, all others were mere angels or divine servants. Even Aten was merely a part of the immortal hosts, but he was nothing compared to the father of all creation.

"Lord," said the grand vizier, "as you know, a pharaoh is divinity on Earth. You are the current divinity. Praise be to King Tutankhaten whose name means 'living image of Aten.' Three short years ago, your father ruled this land. As divinity on Earth, he failed his primary charge to support Maat on Earth to maintain order in the face of chaos. As we know, chaos is death—death for Kemet, death for all life, and death for all creation. Even Lord Aten—your namesake—would appreciate these facts."

"So, what are you saying?" asked the young king. "That my name is an abomination? That I am not worthy because I have been named after Aten rather than Amun?"

"No, my Lord," replied the grand vizier, hastily. "We will all follow you wherever you lead. Our fate is tied to your guidance. If you tell us to go to war, we will go. If you tell us to die, we will die. For the good of all Kemet is more important than the life of one individual."

"Even the life of this one, nine-year-old boy?"

"No, your eminence." The grand vizier took a deep breath. This was going to be more difficult than he had imagined. "You are no longer merely a boy. You are Kemet. Your life and well-being must be protected at all cost. Without you, there is no Kemet."

"If that is the case," said the young king, slowly, "then why was my stepmother poisoned?"

The grand vizier's face grew red. A volley of shocked expressions ran through the crowd of administrators surrounding the king. Suddenly, the naked reality confronted all of them that this young king could have all of them put to death. He could wipe the slate clean and establish a new set of advisors.

The grand vizier was wise in his years and knew that this young king had seen great turmoil in the land because of the disagreements with the policies of Akhenaten, the boy's father. He knew that he needed to take the darkness on directly.

"My Lord," he said quietly, "you have the power and authority to put all of us to death."

Those words shocked many of the advisors present. Some merely held their collective breaths and waited for the boy king's response.

"If we offend you," continued the grand vizier, "in any way, you need to take decisive action against that which damages the order of things. The old vizier was crazy, driven mad by chaos. But that's what happens when a king or queen leads Kemet toward chaos. It is your right to do that. You can utterly destroy Kemet, for Kemet is yours and yours alone. As long as we remain sane and free of chaos, we will follow your commands to the letter, even if they lead us all to chaos."

The young king took a deep breath and turned away from the grand vizier. He scanned the faces of the others, gauging their expressions. On some, he saw suppressed terror, but a resolve to obey. On others, he saw merely the quiet attitude of a courtly toady—a pasted-on smile and shrewd, penetrating eyes.

The new pharaoh turned again and faced the grand vizier. "What do you recommend?"

"Over the first few years of your long reign," replied the grand vizier, taking an even deeper breath before continuing, "I recommend that you return Kemet to the rule of Maat, goddess of order. Our land has been torn by this diversion to Aten. First, you could change your name, for that is your right as Lord of all Kemet. Something to honor Amun—the one true god."

"So," said the king, "change my name to Tutankhamun—'living image of Amun'—a god which has no image?"

"If you wish, my Lord."

"What else?"

"I recommend that we move the capital back to Waset so that our people can feel that order has been restored to the land."

"Very well," said the young king. "I will think about what you have suggested. I appreciate your candor and your wisdom. All of Kemet is blessed that it has such a strong and wise counselor. Now, leave me, so that I may think on these things."

A Return to Order

Soon, the entire city of Akhetaten was abandoned and everything there fell into ruin.

When nine years later the teenage pharaoh died, his grand uncle, Ay, took the throne. That man ruled for four brief years.

When Ay died, the chief commander of the army took over. His name was Horemheb, an appellation which meant "Horus is in jubilation." This new king ruled for fourteen years and spent a good portion of it destroying every monument left by Akhenaten. The building materials were used instead for more traditional monuments. Because of this, modern historians almost never found out about Akhenaten and his family. In fact, the king lists handed down from one pharaoh to the next showed Amenhotep III followed directly by Horemheb.

When Horemheb died, he made sure to hand the rule of the empire over to his vizier—a man named

Paramesse. The vizier took the throne with the name Ramesses I—grandfather of Ramesses the Great.

Chapter 8 — Ramesses the Great

All of Egyptian history seemed to lead up to the great Ozymandias—Ramesses II (c1303–1213 BC). Everything which came after him did not measure up to his stature. He was the King of Kings—the one about whom the poet would write, some 3,000 years later: "Look on my Works, ye Mighty, and despair!" Yet, his power eventually crumbled to dust.

Ramesses II's father, Seti I, reclaimed much of the territory lost under Akhenaten. He had even taken back Kadesh (a town in Syria) and the region of Amurru, both conquered decades before by the Hittites. But the Egyptians under Seti once again lost

Kadesh, because it was so close to the Hittite homelands and not easily controlled from the Egyptian capital.

In his second year on the throne, Ramesses II (reign 1279–1213 BC) was faced with a threat to commerce from the Sherden sea pirates. Other nations had been sending ships rich with cargo to Egypt for trade, but the pirates saw this as an opportunity for easy prosperity. The king placed ships and troops all along the Egyptian coast at strategic locations. He used merchant ships as bait, but each was filled with soldiers. The pirates took the bait and suffered their own enslavement.

Ramesses retook Amurru from the Hittites during his fourth year.

The king built a new capital city of Pi-Ramesses and included factories which would manufacture the tools of war—chariots, swords, shields, and more.

During his seventh year, Ramesses returned to the North to battle the Hittites once again. Though his campaign proved successful, Kadesh and Amurru were soon returned to Hittite control. In the tenth year, Ramesses attempted once again to reclaim that northern territory, but failed.

Relations between the two countries remained uneasy for several years thereafter.

Mursili III ruled the Hittite Empire from 1272–1265 BC, but was deposed by his uncle, Hattusili III, because of the younger man's lack of skill and the fact that he let the Assyrians capture their huge territory of Hanigalbat (Mittani). At first Mursili III attempted to regain the throne, but failed. When all hope for him looked lost, he fled to the one place no Hittite would ever go—Egypt.

Hattusili III discovered that Mursili III had gone to Egypt and sent word to the court of Ramesses demanding that his nephew be returned to Hatti. The Egyptian pharaoh denied any knowledge of Mursili III's presence in the lands of the Nile. The Hittite king did not believe Ramesses and threatened war.

In the year 1258 BC—Ramesses' 21st year—both kings agreed to draw up a peace treaty. Neither side seemed well equipped to pursue a perpetual war over Kadesh, and neither side was willing merely to walk away from the city or its surrounding territory.

The World's First Known Peace Treaty

A tall, middle-aged man crossed the room and looked down at the table where the grand vizier stood. The vizier indicated the scroll on the table and bowed his head to the one who had approached. This was no ordinary man of 45 years. He was trim, with a bearing of confidence and power. When he moved, everyone in the room noticed. This was the King of Kings and he was being humbled by today's event.

After a few moments, Ramesses II looked up from the table. His eyes drilled into those of the vizier. "You've got to be kidding. I'm not signing this." He glanced at the Hittite representative who stood a few paces behind his vizier. "Really? Egypt sued Hatti for peace? Do you really want to start a war on the eve of peace?" He shook his head. "No! This won't do. It's all wrong. The Hittites sued for peace, not the other way around."

"Your eminence," said the Hittite. "If I may."

"Speak. It may be the last time you do, but if it can prevent war, then you must." He shook his head again and turned away from them.

"What if we have two versions of the treaty?" The Hittite hesitated, and waited a moment to see if his first words invited more.

Ramesses turned, eyes narrowing as if to focus more sharply on the man himself.

The Hittite continued. "We both need to appease our courts and noblemen. We cannot take back a treaty which says that Hatti sued for peace. And I easily understand why you cannot take back one which says that Egypt sued for peace. Both are positions of weakness, and I know that both parties are not weak. But we must keep appearances. If we can both agree to sign a treaty with two versions of wording—everything the same except that which is needed to keep our people happy—then we will have accomplished something truly remarkable."

Ramesses nodded. "I'm beginning to appreciate the notion that diplomats are very much like salesmen in the bazaars. We need to check our valuables when we leave—to make certain we possess all our fingers. I have no doubt your skills at tricking us are mighty." He paused for a moment, then winked at his vizier. Abruptly, he turned and left.

The vizier turned to the startled Hittite and said, "Then it is agreed. Two wordings. All clauses of substance shall be exactly the same, but those which are for show only will have two versions—the Hittite version to show a favorable image of Hatti, and the Egyptian version to show a favorable image of Kemet."

The Hittite took a deep breath, nodded, and offered a guarded smile at what had been accomplished here. These men had created something the world had never before seen. He hoped that this treaty of peace would last.

Chapter 9 — Cleopatra, End of an Epoch

Alexander the Great conquered Egypt in 332 BC. This is why so many of the Egyptian cities of the Classical period had Greek names—Thebes, Memphis, Heliopolis, etc. In addition, the city of Alexandria, Egypt was founded by him. For the last 300 years of Ancient Egypt's existence, the land of the Nile was ruled by those of Greek heritage.

Cleopatra VII was the last of her dynasty—the last ruler of a sovereign, Ancient Egypt. After her, Egypt was merely a province of one empire after another— the Roman Empire(30 BC–AD 400), the Byzantine Empire (400–628), the Sasanian Empire of Persia

(628–639), the Fatimid Caliphate (c650–c1250), the Mamluks (c1250–1517), the Ottoman Empire (1517–1867), and finally as a British protectorate (1882–1952).

With Cleopatra, more than three thousand years of history were coming to an end. Egypt would no longer have a pharaoh after her.

As a young girl of fourteen, Cleopatra (69–30 BC) came to power for the first time, but one of her decisions turned out to be very unpopular. By the time she had turned 21, her younger brother, Ptolemy XIII, had taken her place as sole ruler of Egypt. After a failed rebellion, Cleopatra fled the country.

About the same time, Rome was entangled in a brutal civil war between Julius Caesar and the great Pompey. When Pompey fled to Egypt and asked for assistance, Ptolemy XIII feared the consequences of any action he might take—either helping or shunning the Roman general. One of his advisors, however, suggested a third option which would help Caesar and gain his favor. So, Ptolemy ordered Pompey to be assassinated. When the pharaoh's representative presented Pompey's severed head to Caesar, the Roman was outraged that this Roman consul had been betrayed so brutally.

Caesar took over the Egyptian capital and decided to end the feud between Ptolemy and his sister, Cleopatra.

When Cleopatra heard of this, she returned to Egypt and had her agents roll her up in a carpet so that she could be taken past Ptolemy's guards into the midst of Julius Caesar. Once there, she used her charms to win Caesar's affections. Nine months later, their son, Ptolemy Caesar (47–30 BC), was born.

Both mother and son were taken to Rome as guests of Caesar. They lived there for two years, until Julius Caesar was assassinated (March 15, 44 BC). They both returned to Egypt and later that year, Cleopatra declared that her son, though only three years of age, would be co-ruler with her.

After Caesar's death, Rome was ruled by a triumvirate which included Gaius Octavius (Octavian, adopted son of Julius Caesar), Marcus Antonius (Mark Antony), and Lepidus. When Lepidus was forced into retirement in 36 BC, Octavian controlled the Western provinces, while Antony controlled those in the East. During that period, Mark Antony had three children with Cleopatra.

Imagining the Final Days of Kemet

Nearly three years had passed since the triumvirate had been broken. Octavian grew suspicious of Mark Antony, the leader of the East. When he heard that Mark Antony had declared young Caesarion (Ptolemy Caesar) to be the true heir of Julius Caesar, Octavian naturally felt threatened. He was only an adopted son; Caesarion had the great general's blood running through his veins.

"Your eminence," said the old man, "what you said in the Senate was masterful. Condemning Antony for all of the titles and grants of territory he had given to his relatives—the Senate understands these things. They fear and loathe such selfishness and arrogant nepotism. But remember, everything you do must be with humility and reverence to the traditions of Rome. You cannot be seen to seek power for yourself. You must refuse power. When it is forced upon you, you must accept it reluctantly."

Octavian had been looking out the window onto the moonlit Tyrrhenian Sea. He half heard the wisdom of his old counselor. The other half of his thoughts were on the far end of the Mediterranean, wondering how he could destroy Marcus Antonius and his evil bitch queen, Cleopatra.

"How do I kill them, Claudius?" He turned from the window and looked into the eyes of his advisor. Octavian was 29; his advisor was 69.

"You don't," said old man. "You can never be seen to have killed them. You must always be seen as magnanimous, strong, but forgiving. A few will hate you for showing leniency. You cannot please everyone. But the majority of Rome—especially the patricians and senators—will appreciate the strength it takes to show mercy."

"If I cannot kill them, then how will I ever be rid of them? This claim by Marcus Antonius threatens my very existence. If Caesarion ever gains a strong following in Rome, I'm as good as dead."

The old man paused for a moment, choosing his words carefully. "You can stick your sword into Antonius, but the world must believe that the man fell on his own sword out of shame for his failures. His queen can be slaughtered, but the world must believe that she chose to commit suicide instead of suffering capture."

"I see," said Octavian. "There is one version of reality—the private and true version—and there is the other version for all of history."

Claudius nodded. "You must plan your moves carefully. Build the public outrage against Antonius, as you've been doing. Make him extremely unpopular. Then work your way toward a military conflict that you are certain to win. Rome loves a winner, especially if it is one of their own."

Over the next few years, Octavian patiently built outrage and carefully maneuvered Marcus Antonius into a battle he couldn't win.

And the young emperor-to-be followed his advisor's words. He cornered Marcus Antonius, killing him outright, but only amongst his most trusted soldiers.

"Give me his sword," said Octavian. "See?" He took the dead man's sword and shoved it into the same wound that had dispatched him to Elysium. "He committed suicide, falling on his own sword, instead of facing justice. This is how much of a coward was the man who stood against Rome."

All of the officers looking on nodded in agreement. They knew that politics needed to be involved here, every bit as much as warfare.

Later, when Octavian's forces closed in on the Egyptian capital, he pulled his most trusted officers aside and spoke to them in confidence.

"Men, just as Marcus Antonius fell on his sword, his queen must choose the asp for her own death."

"But sire," said one of his generals, "dying by cobra bite takes hours in excruciating pain. She would know that. I doubt—"

"But most people won't know that," replied Octavian. "We need to tell a colorful tale of her ending, otherwise people will suspect the worst of me. That truly would be a tragedy. No, we tell the story that she chose to put her hand in a basket filled with the poisonous vipers. People's thoughts will be so shocked and repulsed, they won't be able to get the picture out of their minds."

"Yes, your eminence," replied the general.

"The age of pharaohs has come to an end," said Octavian. "The age of Roman rule and senatorial wisdom has arrived." He didn't dare speak of himself as emperor. He remembered all too well what had happened to his uncle and adoptive father, Julius Caesar, some fourteen years earlier. He would wait patiently for power to be forced upon him. And he would accept it reluctantly.

Soon, Octavian became known as Augustus Caesar. Though he never proclaimed himself to be emperor, he was that in every way possible throughout the remainder of his life—emperor of Rome and the new ruler of Egypt as a province of that empire.

Conclusion

Modern Egypt looks nothing like its ancient self. It has become a pawn in a far larger game. But if history teaches us anything, we need to remain aware of the patterns of history itself, lest we repeat past mistakes. By reading this work on Egyptian mythology, you have hopefully gained a fascinating perspective on the gods, monsters, and heroes of Egypt's past. Egypt has had a colorful history. From the deepest reaches of pre-dynastic prehistory through all of antiquity, Egypt has arguably seen more history and culture than any other patch of land on Earth.

If you have enjoyed this book, please be sure to leave a review and a comment! I will take the time to read it. Thank you very much.

Can you help me?

If you enjoyed this book, then I'd really appreciate it if you would post a short review on Amazon. I read all the reviews myself so that I can continue to provide books that people want.

Please visit the link below if you'd like to leave a review:

https://www.amazon.com/review/create-review/B0745ZYX63

Or go directly to the book page on amazon:

https://www.amazon.com/B0745ZYX63

Thanks for your support!

Preview of Egyptian Mythology
Captivating Stories of the Gods,
Goddesses, Monsters and Mortals

Introduction: Egypt in Context

Mention the name "Egypt" to most anyone with at least a high school education and it conjures up pictures of the desert, the Nile, palm trees, pyramids and the Sphinx. Today, Egypt is a third-world country rich with petroleum (16% of the nation's economy in 2011), tourism (20%) and industry (20%). The country even makes a substantial income (3%) from their Suez Canal which allows shipping to bypass having to go around Africa for transporting goods between Europe and the Far East.

For the first three thousand years of humanity's shared history, Egypt played a pivotal role in the affairs of man. Its Nile Valley and Delta were one of the cradles of civilization where an organized and settled society was born. The other cradles were found in,

- Mesopotamia—surrounding the Tigris and Euphrates Rivers (modern Iraq),

- Indus Valley—surrounding the Indus River (modern Pakistan),

- China—surrounding the Yellow River,

- Central Andes (modern Peru), and

- Mesoamerica.

Of these six, Egypt and Mesopotamia compete for first place. Both of these regions also vie for first as the birthplace of writing. The Andes and Indus River regions came hundreds of years later. And the earliest known inklings of civilization came more than a thousand years later in China and Mesoamerica.

What's to Come

The book is broken into three parts:

1. Fantastic Images—Ancient Egyptian myths and legends as we know them today.

2. Factual History—Covering pre-history through classical antiquity.

3. Unraveling Myth—Looking at Egyptian mythology from a fresh perspective.

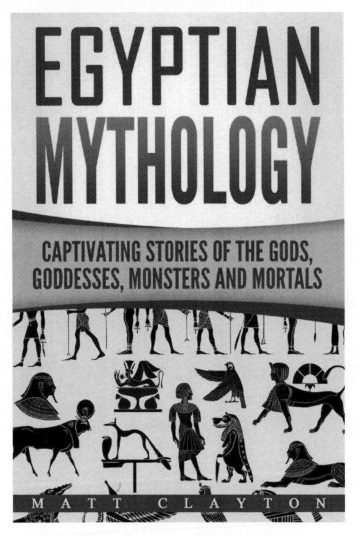

Check out this book!

Preview of Greek Mythology

A Captivating Guide to the Ancient Gods, Goddesses, Heroes and Monsters

Introduction

Any book on ancient mythology gives us a glimpse into the minds of civilization's pioneers. They were the brave adventurers who explored the unknown territory of possibilities. For them, civilization was yet a mysterious realm with countless directions to go.

The broad arc of this book takes us from the dim beginnings of creation as seen in the Greek mythology. We move through the birth of Titans, their overthrow by the Olympian gods, the gods' dealings with mortals like Paris of Troy, the destruction of

Atlantis, Jason and the Golden Fleece, the Trojan War, and into historical times.

This book includes some of the standard views of Greek myth and history, but also tantalizes your imagination with the possibilities that lay behind myth and legend. We won't cover every possible version of every myth, but by the time you're finished with this book, you will have a good appreciation for the nature of Greek mythology and the gods, monsters, and heroes which populate it.

Chapter 1 — Uranus: Betrayal by Cronus

In the very beginning, Chaos (void) ruled the universe. It was the great nothingness. Boring? Of course. Perhaps the sheer blandness of all that empty nothingness forced Gaia (goddess of Earth) to spring into existence from all that emptiness. Close behind, Chaos gave birth to Tartarus (god of the underworld), Eros (god of fertility), Erebus (god of darkness) and Nyx (goddess of night).

Gaia (mother Earth) was so full of fertility that she gave birth to two other primordial gods without having to mate with anyone. Of course, Chaos had no gender, and the universe was relatively empty. Her two sons were named Uranus (god of heaven) and Pontus (god of the ocean).

Feeling lonely, Gaia took her son, Uranus, as her mate. Each night, her son would lay on top of her and mate with her. From these repeated unions, she gave birth to several Titans and monsters. These included Cronus (sometimes spelled Kronos), Oceanus, Tethys, Rhea, Hyperion, Theia, Cruis, Themis, Coeus, Mnemosyne, Iapetus, Phoebe, the Cyclopes, and the Hecatonchires.

To the Greeks, heaven was selfish. He had a unique relationship with Earth and assumed that he was king of the gods. Was that arrogance? Was it that the other gods didn't care who called themselves "king?" Perhaps so, because nothing is mentioned of any conflict until Uranus started to abuse his children.

Uranus gave selfish love to his mate (his mother and wife). There was passion, but there was also disgust for the children his wife gave him. The youngest of these—the Hecatonchires and Cyclopes—he ended up locking away in his uncle, Tartarus (underworld)—far below the surface of Gaia.

For some reason, Uranus considered these youngest to be particularly hideous. The Hecatonchires, for instance, were three man-like giants, but each with a hundred hands, fifty heads, and massive strength. The Cyclopes were three giants, each with one eye in the centers of their foreheads.

Cousins, Nieces, and Nephews

Over the ages, the universe became more crowded with additional gods and goddesses. The primordials Erebus and Nyx got together and made Aether (God of Light) and Hemera (Goddess of Day). The Titans had some fun, too. Oceanus took his sister, Tethys, and they together created Amphrite, Dione, Metis, Pleione, Thetis and hundreds of additional, second generation Titans.

Iapetus married one of his nieces—the Oceanid, Clymene—and they together created Atlas, Prometheus, and several others.

Hyperion took his sister, Theia, and they created Helios (sun), Eos (dawn) and Selene (moon).

Coeus married his sister, Phoebe ("shining") and they created Leto who later became the mother of Artemis and Apollo.

Gaia Fed Up with Abuse

Mother Earth became sickened by the abuses of Uranus. She didn't want any more children by that selfish, self-centered tyrant.

From her own body, she plucked a shard of flint and fashioned a great sickle. But the only harvest she had in mind was to reap from Uranus his testicles. This is an ironic concept. Everything else about the earliest gods of the universe—the primordials—is devoid of anything anthropomorphic (man-like). But here, Uranus has the very human physical attribute of male testes.

Perhaps Gaia was a coward for not doing the deed herself, or perhaps she felt that one of her sons would be more capable of finishing the task. She ended up asking all her sons to take up the great sickle. But even her sons were too cowardly to face up to the Great God King Uranus—all except Cronus.

Cronus was the youngest of the first generation Titans. In other words, he was only slightly older than the brothers imprisoned in Tartarus. Perhaps being the youngest who remained free made him struggle harder to keep up with his older siblings. And perhaps, being only slightly older than his imprisoned brothers made him more aware of his own vulnerabilities. Maybe these traits gave him sufficient ambition to overcome any fear.

But Cronus was clever and shrewd. He wasn't one to jump into a task blindly. After all, he did want to survive the attack on his father—heaven itself. So, Cronus hid and ambushed his father, completing the castration and spilling the god's blood onto the Earth (Gaia). From the blood sprang the Giants, the Meliae, and the Furies (Erinyes). Later, the Meliae would give birth to the earliest form of humans.

Tired and disgusted from the task, Cronus tossed his father's genitals into the ocean (Pontus). Such potent energy remained in the godly organ that the sea whipped up an extreme froth (sea foam, *aphros*) and from it was born Aphrodite Ourania (goddess of spiritual love).

Uranus groaned in agony at the betrayal and condemned all of those of his children who were currently visible—the ones not in Tartarus—calling his sons, "Titanes Theoi," which means "straining gods." From this curse, we get the word "Titan."

With Uranus made impotent, the Hecatonchires and Cyclopes were freed from Tartarus. Gaia was relieved that her youngest sons were finally liberated.

Cronus, feeling the ambitious pride swell within him, took advantage of the situation and claimed the universe as his own. He now became the new king of the gods.

But Cronus had not performed the task requested by his mother and grandmother, Gaia, in order to free his younger brothers. Quite the contrary, Cronus despised the Cyclopes and Hecatonchires as much as his father and brother, Uranus, did. At the first opportunity, Cronus put his six younger brothers back in Tartarus, greatly angering his mother at the betrayal.

Despite his arrogance and cruelty, in some respects, Cronus's rule was viewed as a Golden Age. During his time as king of the gods, the Meliae gave birth to the first humans. These men lived for thousands of years but maintained a youthful appearance. This was a time of tranquility and nobility of spirit, and the young, fragile race of humans mingled with the gods.

With his scythe, Cronus became associated with the harvest and its celebration. His rule was filled with abundance.

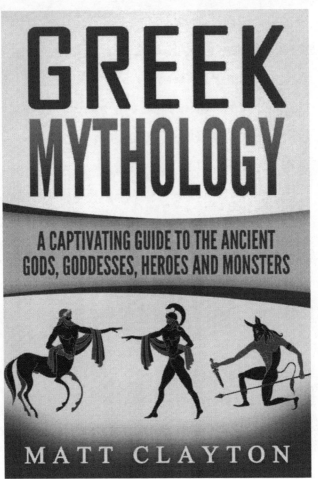

Check out this book!

Preview of Norse Mythology

Captivating Stories of the Gods, Sagas and Heroes

Introduction: Sources and Overview

This book gives an overview of Norse mythology, telling some of the stories of the gods, giants and other creatures of that lost era before history began.

Though the world came to know of the Norse and their legends through Roman interaction about the time of Christ, most of what we came to know was handed down from folk tales gathered by native writers like Snorri Sturluson (c. 1179–1241). This was from a time when the Norse had already been converted to Christianity. Some of what Sturluson wrote was clearly influenced by Christian beliefs of the time. As with all sources, we have to assume at least a little bit of bias was involved. The age of belief in the Norse gods had ended. We can only guess how much of those old beliefs were left out because they may have been incompatible with the new beliefs of Christendom. Sturluson gathered the tales in a work now known as the *Prose Edda*.

Several anonymous writers of the pre-Christian era created poems which have collected in what is now called the *Poetic Edda*. These pre-date Sturluson's work and thus are far more likely to give us insights into the thinking and attitudes of the early Norse people.

Danish scholar Saxo Grammaticus gave us a Latin language version of Danish history, *Gesta Danorum,* written in the twelfth century. But even earlier, we have more matter-of-fact writing of Roman historian Tacitus in the first century, discussing the tribes of the region they called Germania.

As with most stories, it's best to start at the beginning. And as with any story of gods, we start with the Norse version of creation.

Chapter 1—Norse Creation Story

Like most cultures, the rugged folk of the North have their own myth of creation. For them, it started with Ymir, ancestor of all the giants of Jötunheim. Later, Odin and his two brothers, Vili and Vé, defeated Ymir and formed the world from the giant's carcass— hair for the trees, bones for the hills, blood for the ocean, skull for the heavens, brains for the clouds and eyebrows for the land of humans called Midgard (Middle Earth or Middle Land).

None of the stories are clear about the origins of the three Aesir gods—Odin and his brothers. In some respects, these three are similar to the Greek gods, the brothers Zeus, Poseidon and Hades, who defeated the Titans and replaced them as rulers of the universe.

The universe became a giant tree called Yggdrasil which grew out of a well called Urd. Within the tree's branches and roots resided the Nine Realms.

The name itself comes from Yggr—"The Terrible One"—a name frequently given to Odin. For the well, the name "Urd" meant "destiny."

Gods of Different Types

First came the giants—wild, uncivilized, and powerful. We will see more of them in chapter 3.

The Vanir are another set of gods in Norse mythology. They are frequently associated with the indigenous folks of the northlands—the first people to fill the void left by the melting glaciers. Those original folk were later overcome by invading Indo-Europeans.

The Aesir gods are sometimes associated with the conquering invaders who overwhelmed and took in the original inhabitants as their subjects.

Other "Creatures"

Land spirits are powerful beings associated with localized areas of land. From all that was written about them, it's hard to draw a clear-cut line between them and the gods. In fact, the line separating land spirits from elves, giants and dwarves is equally as blurred.

The land spirits jealously guard the realms they oversee. They easily take offense when someone mistreats the land, and they dish out curses just as easily as blessings.

Elves are also powerful beings, frequently called "luminous." Freyr, a Vanir god, and honorary Aesir, also seemed to be associated with the elves of Alfheim, possibly even their ruler, for he lived there, instead of in Asgard or Vanaheim. Yet, in some writings the distinction between elves and gods seems clearer and more pronounced.

Dwarves, unlike the common word used in our language, were not short people. At least nothing in the writings of the Norsemen suggests any deficit in height. There was the suggestion of invisibility and perfectly black in appearance. Were they "invisible" because they were black and not easily seen at night?

They called the underground of Svartalfheim their home—a place full of mining and forges. Many of the fine artifacts of civilization, used by both gods and men, were forged by these beings. These artifacts included Mjölnir (Thor's hammer), Skíðblaðnir (Skidbladnir: Freyr's ship with perpetual fair winds), Gungnir (Odin's spear), Gleipnir (the chain which bound evil Fenrir when everything else had failed), and many others. Dwarves don't merely like the darkness; if exposed to the sun's rays, they immediately turn to stone.

On occasion, dwarves have been labeled "black elves," so the line between dwarves and elves remains somewhat unclear, as well. Because of their skill with metals, it's easy to compare the Norse dwarves with the Cyclopes of Greek myth who fashioned great weapons for Zeus, Poseidon, and others. We cannot help but wonder if the Greeks and Norsemen were talking about the same group of people—blacksmiths who learned an ancient art that was lost and then learned again by the humans at a far later age.

The Norns were three females, each with more power over the path of destiny than any other individual in the universe. They made their home in the Well of Urd, below Yggdrasil. In some versions of myth, they controlled destiny by carving runic symbols into the trunk of the great tree. In other versions, they wove a great tapestry with each strand controlling the life of another. One of these females was named Urd (like the well itself), which comes from the word which means "what once was" in Old Norse. Another was called Verdandi ("what is coming into being"). And the last was called Skuld ("what shall be"). Unlike the Greek fates, the destiny woven by the Norns was much more malleable. It left room for brave individuals to change their own destiny.

Valkyries are the choosers of the fallen. They are female spiritual aides to Odin, who carry dead heroes to Valhalla—a sort of heaven for brave warriors. In more modern times, such as with Wagner's music—*Ride of the Valkyries*—these divine females have been made to look noble. But they have a darker side. They also choose who will be slain. In fact, they have been portrayed on numerous occasions as downright bloodthirsty. They are extensions of Odin, doing his bidding as if they were appendages of his.

Disir are female spirits who acted as guardians of specific individuals, groups, or places. The Valkyries were sometimes called Odin's Disir. And like the Valkyries, the Disir could be warlike in nature.

Ask and Embla were the first humans. When two tree trunks washed ashore onto the land which the gods had only recently raised from the ancient waters, Odin and his brothers gave them *önd* (breath or spirit), *óðr* (inspiration or ecstasy), and something called *lá* which has not to this day been translated. The two humans were given Midgard to rule. The man's name comes from Old Norse, *askr* ("ash tree") and the wife's name meant "water pot." Symbolically, these two names paralleled the functioning of Yggdrasil and Urd—the Great Tree and the Water Well of creation. This imagery emphasizes the fact that one cannot long exist without the other—Yggdrasil and Urd, man and woman.

Sleipnir was an eight-legged horse belonging to Odin. Upon Sleipnir, the chief god made his numerous trips up and down Yggdrasil to visit the Nine Realms, always searching for more knowledge. Sleipnir came into being after Loki had shape shifted into a mare and later became pregnant by a giant's stallion.

Hugin and Munin were two helping spirits in the form of ravens. Their names meant "thought" and "desire," respectively. As you might have guessed, these two high-flying eyes were helpers of Odin, keeping him informed about events far and wide. Like the Valkyries, Hugin and Munin were semi-autonomous, but also extensions of Odin himself.

Berserkers *(berserkir)* and Ulvhethnar *(úlfheðnar)* were two forms of warrior shamans, each with their own totem animal. Berserkers ("bear shirts") naturally chose the bear as their symbol. Ulvhethnar ("wolf hide"), on the other hand, chose the wolf as their icon. Both would go into battle, fearlessly not wearing armor or clothes—only an animal mask and pelts—and madly attacking the enemy with wild abandon. In fact, this is where we get the English word *berserk*. In the age of Vikings, Berserkers and Ulvhethnar would inevitably frighten their enemies by their insane actions. It was commonly believed that these warrior shamans would remain unharmed by both iron and fire. Certainly, a warrior's glee for battle would make many a defender timid, even if only for a few seconds. In battle, a few seconds is all that is needed to win in a one-on-one struggle.

The End

Unlike the Greek's and their mythology, the Norse had the end of times already figured out. Their "twilight of the gods" was called Ragnarök—a time when most of the gods would die, and the worlds would suffer greatly all manner of cataclysms. But because of their view of time and nature as cyclic, this big ending would also be a new beginning.

Geography

The realms were loosely divided into two key types—*innangard* and *utangard*. Innangard—"inside the fence"—was considered to include all lands which were law-abiding, orderly and civilized. Utangard—"outside the fence"—on the other hand, referred to realms which were rough, wild, ancient and chaotic.

Only Asgard and Midgard had names which contained the -gard suffix, and thus referred to fortified places of order, protected from the chaos. Asgard was the realm of the Aesir, while Midgard was the realm of humanity. We will see more of these two places and the other seven worlds in the next chapter.

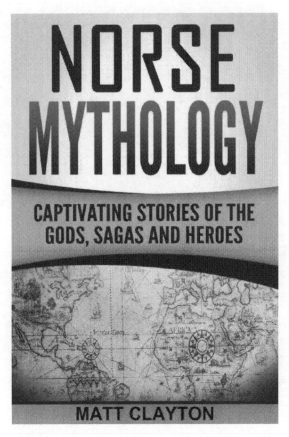

Check out this book!

Make sure to check out more books in the captivating history series!

www.amazon.com/author/mattclayton

www.amazon.com/author/captivatinghistory

Free Bonus from Captivating History (Available for a Limited time)

Hi History Lovers!

Now you have a chance to join our exclusive history list so you can get your first history ebook for free as well as discounts and a potential to get more history books for free! Simply visit the link below to join.

Captivatinghistory.com/ebook

Also, make sure to follow us on:
Twitter: @Captivhistory
Facebook: Captivating History: @captivatinghistory

16102347R00149

Printed in Great Britain
by Amazon